What church leaders **really** need to know

What church leaders **really** need to know

• • • • • • • • • • •

A Practical How-To Guide

ROBERT H. NAYLOR

THE PILGRIM PRESS
Cleveland

The Pilgrim Press
700 Prospect Avenue
Cleveland, Ohio 44115
thepilgrimpress.com

Library of Congress Cataloging-in-Publication Data

Naylor, Robert H., 1946–
What church leaders really need to know : a practical how-to guide / Robert H. Naylor.
pages cm
Includes bibliographical references.
ISBN 978-0-8298-1974-8 (alk. paper)
1. Christian leadership—Handbooks, manuals, etc. I. Title.
BV652.1.N38 2013
253—dc23

2013020918

1 2 3 4 5 6 7 8 9

Contents

Preface

When their class reading assignments were handed out, skeptical and confused looks covered the faces of many of the seminarians who were taking my "Parish Practically" class. I had been asked to teach a short session course on the realities of parish ministry at the seminary from which I had graduated. Perhaps my selection had something to do with previously having been awarded recognition for excellence in parish ministry. Or maybe it was because I was generous in my alumni contributions to the divinity school. I prefer to believe the former. But for whatever reason, as the guest lecturer and adjunct professor it was my responsibility to select the tomes to be read on the subject at hand. The inquisitive looks might have had something to do with what some would consider the less than academically weighty book selections. The Quaker clergyman and professor at Earlham College Tom Mullen and the beloved priest-professor Henri Nouwen seemed to be strange bedfellows. In most of his writings, Mullen used humor to carry very practical and important messages about faith, human relationships, and the institutional church. Nouwen was known for his meditative, reflective sense of spirituality. I felt that Mullen's *Mountaintops and Molehills: Essays in Haphazard Theology* and Nouwen's *Creative Ministry* blended together well for a course that was to help students wrestle with the questions "How do I see myself as a parish minister?" and "What are the day-to-day realities in being a professional leader in this institution, the local church, or the Body of Christ?" (as the Apostle Paul called it).

The underlying reason for my being asked to become an esteemed —that designation was the school's adjective, and I have to admit it grows on you—short-term professor was that the seminary leadership was hearing a common cry from some in their student body and seminary administrators that there was a lack of course options in the area of "practical theology." There were many offerings that taught biblical exegesis or the great theologians such as Barth, Brunner, and, Calvin. But no one focused a single course on how to balance professional and family life or how to manage an annual financial stewardship campaign. Graduates were given voluminous information on church history and theories of pastoral counseling. Yet few or no opportunities were provided to understand how to oversee a wedding rehearsal or guide a family planning for a funeral or write and deliver an age-appropriate children's meditation or deal with a conflict at a church leadership board meeting.

These realities had made my required reading decisions for the class difficult. As I combed my library and the catalogs of national Christian book publishers for seminal books in the practice of ministry, I found few resources that would give a true picture of the basic realities of parish ministry. Few would actually help to shape the soul of one who would eventually accept the call to serve a local church. Amid my struggles to find the reading material that would give a true picture of parish life, I found myself sliding my fingers up and down the spine of a small book with cartoon figures on the front. It was Mullen's book *Mountaintops and Molehills*. The opening pages of the well-worn paperback led me to a moment of insight and of laughter. Mullen used the image of the children of Israel in the wilderness seeking the Promised Land as a metaphor for parish ministry. How could one deliver the Good News within the context of the local church? He correctly understood the depth of the biblical text when he highlighted that the journey would be fraught with God-encounter moments, with foolish behaviors and wrong turns. He compared this to the journey of all Christians in the local church and concluded that there is little systematic theology that gives an honest understanding of the faith journey of most Christians and most churches. All theology, particularly in the local parish, is "haphazard theology." Mullen's essays gave an honest, human, and humorous picture of the journey of faith as witnessed in the parish setting. One of his most salient comments came when he was reflecting on church committee meetings. While praising volunteers, he wrote: "When all was said and done, usually more was said than done."[1] Seminaries have many courses on systematic theology but need courses for those entering the parish ministry, a class in "haphazard" theology. This was the class I was called to create and teach.

The second syllabus book that caught my attention was a diminutive but prodigious book, *Creative Ministry,* by Nouwen. By appearances Nouwen's long essay was no competition for the thick and sometimes multivolume books assigned by tenured professors. Father Nouwen reflected on five core ministry tasks in the local parish: teaching, preaching, individual pastoral care, organizing, and celebrating. Then almost subliminally he challenged readers to take the time for spiritual discernment to see if they were truly called to serve in this setting.[2] This book is meant to help those called to local church ministry to understand the personal gifts that are essential for dynamic and faithful leadership, leadership that can build up the Body of Christ. It also seeks to offer basic insights into being a leader in all aspects of this ministry. It is written for my colleagues in local church ministry:

- who want to find ways to refresh and energize their ministry
- who want to consider some creative ideas for a particular facet of their ministry
- who are in the discernment process or who are in seminary and want to understand the day-to-day realities of parish ministry and ways to address them
- who are committed lay leaders and are in need of detailed plans for overseeing their ministry
- who want to find the humor in the foibles of parish ministry and the personal joy that is at the heart of dynamic ministry

Within these pages are concrete and creative approaches offered for all facets of ministry: pastoral care, worship, faith development, community life, wider mission, administration, and finance. Along with sounding a call for personal discernment, this book offers advice as a how-to manual. It seeks to offer universal understanding about dynamic leadership that transcends denominational labels. The call for imagination in leadership and creativity in ministry touches on many of the insights of the emergent church movement. Much of what is shared here comes from many joy-filled, spirit-lifting, and, some have said, successful years in multistaff parishes, in a national staff position that focused on clergy development and support and in judicatory ministries with small-membership churches. This book is about a love affair with the local parish church.

At the beginning of each chapter there are Body Building Exercises intended to help you, the reader, gain deeper insight from the chapter. Each chapter closes with devotional insight and a prayer for personal spiritual growth. It is my hope that these resources for spiritual nurture will be used often as you go about your ministry.

Naturally there are autobiographical examples from my four decades in ministry. They are not included for adulation, but rather education. The stories are meant to ground this book in reality. All who pastor local churches have similar stories. They are used to elucidate some of the insights that are offered and to remind us that the church is a human institution with divine intentions.

It is my prayer that in some small way I will empower readers to more clearly understand the haphazard theology that is alive in the local church setting. And I sincerely hope that you will learn to love being the leader on the journey to the Promised Land that each local church seeks. I pray that the Spirit will free you to be creative in that ministry in building up the Body of Christ.

I was surprised to learn that a large majority of the students in that seminary class found my book selections to be filled with some of the most meaningful and useful information needed for their ministries in a parish. I hope that you also find this book to be an equally beneficial resource.

My many partners in ministry made this book possible, specifically:

My parents, Anna and Raymond, who required church attendance and taught me without saying a word what it meant to follow Jesus.

My wife, Gretchen, who has shared in the journey of ministry in quiet yet very obvious ways and who loved me when needed and humbled me when needed.

My sons, Adam and Andrew, who loved me in spite of my haphazard parenting and who have made their mother and me proud in the way they live out their Christian values in their families, in their work, and in the churches they attend.

My mentor Dr. Al Bartholomew, who challenged me to reconsider parish ministry when I wanted to avoid it.

My many colleagues who laughed and cried and created with me something that looked like faithful ministry.

And, of course, thousands of lay persons who loved and accepted me as their pastor in spite of my frailties and proclivity to overwhelm them with the circus of faith that I created.

To all I dedicate this book

As J. S. Bach often said:
Soli Deo Gloria
To God alone the glory!

1

Clergy Identity

"Hey, Messiah, the Diaper Needs Changing"

Body Building Exercises

- Write down four basic characteristics that best describe you.
- Reflect on how these characteristics could be an asset or detriment to your ministry.
- Talk with a trusted family member or friend about these characteristics and how they see them playing out in your ministry.
- Are there areas for growth in your ministry that require your attention?

I am beginning this book with people. Programs are essential in getting the Good News out, but dynamic ministry requires people to spread the Good News: you, I, and anyone else who feels the call from God to lead a community of faith. And the truth is that if local church ministry is to be fruitful, it requires people with particular personal and professional gifts. There is a humorous reflection that gets at the heart of the matter. There was once a very devout farmer who loved God very much and became a pastor of a local church. It seems his leadership skills were called into question by a majority of the church he was serving. He sought the advice of a trusted clergy colleague. In the midst of their heartfelt discussion he related the story of his call. "I was out in the field one day. I had become disenchanted with my life and suddenly I noticed two clouds in the sky forming the letters P and C. I knew it was a sign from God that I should preach Christ." After a lengthy silence his trusted friend looked at him and said, "You can preach Christ anywhere. And did you ever think the P–C meant plant corn?"

This chapter—and of course this book—is meant not only for those considering a call to ordained ministry but also for those who are serving in parish settings and feel the need to periodically reflect on their ministry and make the course corrections that will give renewed vitality to their ministry.

There have been numerous studies on the *personal characteristics and personality types* that are best suited for professional leadership in parish ministry. Roy Oswald and Otto Kroeger of the Alban Institute have used Myers-Briggs personality-type studies to ascertain what appear to be the most compatible types for ordained ministry. Oswald and Kroeger's findings highlighted three types that seemed best suited for effective leadership in the Body of Christ. It is evident that an extroverted personality type would have the greatest opportunity for success. The study found that the strongest personality type is an ENFJ (extroversion, intuition, feeling, judging):

> ENFJs are the benevolent "pedagogues" of humanity. They have tremendous charisma by which many are drawn into their nurturant tutelage and grand schemes. Many ENFJs have tremendous power to manipulate others with their phenomenal interpersonal skills and unique salesmanship. But it's usually not meant as manipulation—ENFJs believe in their dreams, and see themselves as helpers and enablers, which they usually are. While I have known very effective clergy who are moderate introverts, strong relational skills remain an essential asset to being an effective church leader in the building up of the Body of Christ. Church leaders should strongly consider taking a personality test to better know who they are and their personal strengths for ministry.[1]

Secondary to personality characteristics are *professional competencies* essential for dynamic, body building leadership. A helpful barometer for me regarding such competencies comes from my oversight of the United Church of Christ's clergy search and call system. Materials used by the local church in seeking a new pastor include a leadership expectation list. There are forty-four competency desires listed, from which twelve are to be selected by a church search and call committee. The list includes a diverse mixture of personal attributes and professional skills. While it is to a degree true that every church is seeking a messiah, there would appear to be a coalescence of agreement around several expectations:

- The person has a strong faith while being open to the varying faith journeys of others.
- The person has a depth of caring that leads to close, interpersonal relationships that come through personal contacts, visitations, and attentive listening.
- The person is effective in the preparation and leadership of worship.
- The person is trustworthy and keeps confidences.
- The person is effective in teaching the essence of the biblical message through study and prayer.
- The person is mature and has a sense of direction in his or her ministry.

Numerous studies have been done and competency codes have been written that combine leadership qualities and professional competencies. Most reaffirm the list distilled above: spiritually mature, professionally ethical, relational, adaptable, competent in worship leadership. The list is endless, and so the challenges of leadership are great. In consulting with one local church, I was told by a seasoned parishioner that if you want to know what a minister's job description is, "Go visit ninety-six-year-old Marge. She's an eighty-year member. She'll give you the job description." I took the advice. Marge was not shy in responding to my inquiries about leadership. "Bob, you know we want Jesus himself, but we'll settle for someone who shows that God loves us. If our new minister exudes the grace of God, we'll give him a pass on an occasional bad sermon. We've had clergy who see us as the enemy. We want our next pastor to see us as family."

A distillation of resource materials on church leadership highlights six key attributes of a Body of Christ–building leader:

1. humility with a healthy insecurity
2 a positive spirit
3. faithful seeking
4. integrity
5. patient dreaming
6. a hearty sense of humor

1. Humility with a Healthy Insecurity

It is no accident that in the Sermon on the Mount Jesus began with allusions to humility: poverty of spirit and meekness. Even Paul, the strident and often arrogant architect of our faith's theological underpinnings, admitted to weakness and having a thorn in his flesh. Humility is the gift that admits to not having all the answers; that listens first and speaks after hearing; that knows deep down inside that *I* cannot make it alone; that realizes *I* am a wounded healer.

On the basis of focused study on the morale of clergy and in dealing with the chasm of divisions between clergy and laity in conflicted churches, it would appear that often a primary cause of divisiveness is the personal power needs of the church leader. The old model of the pastor as authority figure has been challenged, and those who have adopted a more collegial, partnership style with laity have seen their ministries flourish.

Beware! The leadership of a local church can be seductive for those without a healthy dose of humility. It is a profession where we are daily shown appreciation and even adulation. "I found your sermon thought provoking. I'd love a copy of it." "Thanks for coming to visit me when I was in the hospital." "I know you have some good advice on being the parent of a teenager; I'd appreciate your insights." It's a profession where people come with hurting souls to seek our support. They trust us with the deepest intimacies of their lives. Unless we stay spiritually and personally grounded we can become "legends in our own mind." Humility allows us to separate love given to us because of our roles from misinterpreted love that can lead to unhealthy dependencies and unethical behaviors.

I remember quite vividly when I once was given a strong dose of humility. It had been a great day of rewarding work. My skills of care and creativity had been tested and the accolades had been showered on me. I have to admit there was an unhealthy "Boy, are you good!" taking up residence in my soul. I arrived home late for dinner and my wife was harried because our two young sons were testing her patience by demanding her full attention. I remember pulling into the garage just wanting to sit down and rest and ponder the good that I had done. I began to share the day's victories with my wife as she held a child in each arm. Suddenly she put our older son down and handed me our infant son. Her words were: "Hey, Messiah, the baby's diaper needs changing!" From the holy, clean glow of the day's healings and teaching, I was humbled by the sight of a saintly woman clearly frenzied. Suddenly the messiah was brought back to reality at the sight of an overflowing diaper. It was a humbling moment.

Along with constant remembrance of the opening words of the Beatitudes and the love, support, and honesty of family members, some pastors build networks of respected church leaders and colleagues who will speak the truth in love. An increasing number of pastors have spiritual directors and trusted mentors with whom they keep in regular contact so they do not lose their spiritual center of a humble heart.

2. A Positive Spirit

An affirming and positive spirit is a foundational asset for successful ministry. Dominican priest Matthew Fox authored what was considered by some a heretical book, *Original Blessing*. It was written as a critique of the historic theological dogma of original sin. A very simple synopsis of his thesis is this: God saw creation and all that was created in the divine image as good. Beginning with this presupposition we then approach all that God created with a sense of awe and sacredness. If we begin from an original blessing point of view, our opinion of the human race starts at a positive place. We begin with an affirming approach—a sense of respect because we realize that God saw the creation of humankind as good. We are in awe as we seek the image of God in each person we meet. Many clergy will remember the simple, unsophisticated story of the little boy looking at a large pile of manure and saying with glee, "There's a pony in there somewhere." We all have had those moments when we saw the manure rather than the hoped for pony. Because of sporadic cynicism about lay persons when some have not acted Christian or followed our lead with fervor, we have experienced times when our leadership did little to promote the building up of the Body of Christ. Being affirming and positive in all relationships and reaching for a taste of the dominion of God in the church are critical to dynamic ministry. When we lead with original blessing, spiritual and numerical growth of the local church will follow.

3. Faithful Seeking

Studies show that the most effective clergy see themselves as souls who are seeking, who are far from having all the answers. They have a strong commitment to Jesus as their savior but are still wrestling with issues of faith. They are comfortable in acknowledging that they have been given unique gifts for ministry, and through formal training have identified and honed those gifts. Still, they are forthright in acknowledging they have their own questions and their occasional dark nights of the soul. They periodically find their faith perplexing and the answers it gives cloudy. They see themselves as seekers trying to set the path for other searching souls on this lifelong journey of faith.

On one occasion when I was consulting in a church conflict situation, the council chairwoman said to me in a private moment: "Our pastor is too sure of himself and he comes off as condescending. We're looking for someone who can understand the meanderings of our belief and keep reminding us that if we work at it together the answers are somewhere in this Book. We want someone who can say with commitment, 'Jesus is the answer, but I still have my own questions.'" body builders realize that they have exceptional gifts for ministry but see themselves as seekers along with others in their community.

4. Integrity

Integrity! On occasion I have been asked how I want to be remembered when I die. I usually answer the question in two sentences: "I don't want to rush the time when people are remembering me. But if I must answer, then I want to die with my integrity intact." Adherence to moral and ethical principles, soundness of moral character, honesty—that's the spin the dictionary puts on this sacred word. Trustworthy and always telling the truth, actions that are visible witness to the spoken word—that's integrity. Living with the highest of moral standards—that's integrity. There is something about integrity that says that I will be totally open with you about who I am so that you might have a clear view of the values by which I live. Integrity requires no cover-up; it requires being honest about our strengths and weaknesses, about our wholeness and our brokenness. A life open for inspection leads to profound trust.

Integrity lives itself out through keeping confidences. Secrets shared are secrets kept. Integrity respects differing opinions and actions of others when they are devoid of self-interest. A person of integrity tries with all diligence to live by high standards. But when that person fails to measure up to his or her standards, he or she admits mistakes. What does a person of integrity look like? There is a parabolic story that addresses the question:

> Once there was an emperor who knew he needed to select someone to take his place. Instead of passing his powerful position to one of his family members, he called all the youth of his realm together and gave to each a seed to grow. "Plant, water, and care for this seed," he said, "and bring it back to me one year from now." One young man named Ling took the seed home and cared diligently for it. Yet in spite of his tenacious care it did not grow. The other youths told of the successful growth of their seeds. When the day arrived for the emperor to inspect the hardy plants grown from the seeds, Ling balked, for he did not want to reveal his failure. Nevertheless he was encouraged by his parents to attend the judging. He stood embarrassed amid youth with plants of magnificent size and

> beauty. The emperor called Ling to his side. Then he said, "One year ago today I gave everyone here a seed. I told you to take the seed, plant it, water it, and bring it back to me today. But I gave you all boiled seeds, which would not grow. All of you, except Ling, have brought me beautiful plants. When you found your seed would not grow, you substituted another seed for the one I gave you. Ling was the only one with the courage and honesty to bring me a pot with the original seed in it. He will be the new emperor!"[2]

What more can be said about integrity?

5. Patient Dreaming

The Apostle Paul probably understood it best when he wrote words that most Christians know: "Love is patient and kind." In 1 Corinthians 13 when he began his definition of Christ-like love, he began with those thoughts. It is no accident that patience took the lead. And if there is any profession that needs as its mantra "Love is patient, love is patient . . . ," it is that of pastor or lay leader of a local church.

As might have been the case for some of you, when I arrived at my first parish I assumed the dominion of God would soon arrive in Danbury, Connecticut. The operative word was "soon." After a year it seemed the parish had made little progress with God's or, more accurately, my goal. It seemed the majority of the congregation wasn't in as much of a hurry as I was. And can you believe it, some even had a different vision than I did and were actually impeding God's work. An older church member, who had adopted the young pastor, arrived at my office with a wall poster. A caterpillar looks out sheepishly from its cocoon and beneath it are the words: "Be patient! God isn't finished with me yet." In my frenetic, get-it-done-now moments I remember those words of wisdom. It is an enormous challenge to work on God's time, not our own.

As a pastor of a church in a strongly congregational, lay-based system, I occasionally long for ministry in a hierarchical church. I thought things would get done much more quickly. But I cherish the challenge of having to take a little more time in coming to a decision about the church's future. The church is a community of faith. The word "community" should not be taken lightly. Building agreement or consensus will take some time. And in most cases the result—to use the caterpillar-to-butterfly-image—is more beautiful and flight worthy. Effective leaders need the patience of Moses as he tried to lead the children of Israel on their zigzag path to the Promised Land. The dreams of a new heaven and a new earth surely take time.

6. A Hearty Sense of Humor

I never thought an improvised two-liner would get me a job. It wasn't profound, but to the members of the search committee who were doing the prescreening it smacked of continuing revelation. "How do you look at life and how does that reflect in your ministry?" Without having a chance to filter my words I blurted out, "We are God's Monty Python's Flying Circus! Eighty percent of life is very humorous. Twenty percent of life is to be taken with ultimate seriousness." Then I added an addendum. "And by my demeanor you will know the 20 percent times." For the unschooled in the history of TV humor, *Monty Python's Flying Circus* was a British comedy showing, as most humor does, life's idiosyncrasies. If we cannot stand back from life and see the humor in it, a very important trait of excellence in leadership will be lost: *joy*!

Humor helps us to laugh at ourselves when our human foibles try to have their way with us. Humor helps us to keep perspective on our life together in community. It stifles our pride. It binds us together in our brokenness. It opens the path for forgiveness. It calls us to a dependency on God and one another. In Proverbs 31 the text about the virtuous woman of faith always lingers in my memory. "She laughs at the time to come." Laughter is a sign of trust in God that proclaims that the foolishness of this world can be overcome.

When all is said and done, pastors having a Myers-Briggs personality type ENFJ, as well as its opposite, ISTPs (introversion, sensing, thinking, perceiving), can be effective body builders if they have humble hearts and a commitment to the challenging, fulfilling journey of being a person of faith. We are not called to be the Messiah, but instead to be guides to and partners with other seekers on the chaotic but blessed, haphazard journey to God's Promised Land.

Inspiration

Laughter of course can be strained, cruel, artificial, or merely habitual. It can mask our true feelings. But where it is real, laughter is the voice of faith. . . . Laughter is hope's last weapon. —HARVEY COX[3]

Prayer

God of our ancestors, I give you thanks as I remember those who nurtured my faith and who shaped my character. May their memories always be a guide for my ministry. God of grace and God of glory, when I get too proud, humble me. When I get too weak in spirit, strengthen me. When I take things too seriously, help me join you in a partnership of joyous laughter. Amen.

2

Jesus or Jack-of-All-Trades

A Fresh Look at the Roles Dynamic Leaders Play

Body Building Exercises

- Write down what you believe to be the normative job description for a local church pastor.
- Where do your professional skills match up with this job description? What are your strengths and weaknesses?
- What might you do to improve your skills base as you plan to meet the needs in your weaker skills areas?

Not long ago a member of one of the churches I have served got in touch with me. She had recently been ordained and was now serving a small congregation nestled in the hills of New England. The setting is idyllic, but the church struggles because of its unwillingness to take the risks needed for future growth and vitality. Because of her excellent skills in parish ministry, she was contacted by another church regarding her interest in being considered for their ministerial vacancy. Her initial contact with me came as an e-mail request for me to review the church's job description for the position. Because of my experience in clergy placement and my understanding of the nuances of search resources, she asked for my frank and honest opinion on whether she would be a good fit for the position.

As I read the job description, I was reminded of the words of the search committee chair when I was interviewing for a senior pastor position at a church outside of Hartford, Connecticut. After telling me the three most important ministries that he felt the church needed, he said: "However, another thousand people might have a different opinion." The position description that my Berkshire Hills friend sent included the standard laundry list along with caveats that made them seem less formidable. The subtext was clear: "It's all yours. Enjoy! We'll help out as our schedules permit." That includes worship planning and leadership, all types of pastoral care, faith development for all ages, community and wider church witness, administrator and business plan overseer. Again the Second Coming of Jesus was on the church's mind. A more earthly way of saying what they desired was "You must be a jack-of-all-trades."

The original job description as laid out by Jesus was challenging but less overwhelming than many pastoral leadership job descriptions today: "All authority in heaven and on earth has been given to me. Go therefore and make disciples of all nations, baptizing them in the name of the Father and of the Son and of the Holy Spirit, and teaching them to obey everything that I have commanded you. And remember, I am with you always, to the end of the age" (Mt 28:18–20). While there seemed to be a heavy travel component to the task, it appeared that a little preaching and a little teaching with some attention to the institution of a sacrament was the extent of being a called leader. But the downside was that the salary and benefits package were rather limited. It might entail subsistence living. And when it came to the basic needs of food and shelter, be ready to rely on a little help from your friends. Everything became a bit more expansive after Pentecost:

> Now during those days, when the disciples were increasing in number, the Hellenists complained against the Hebrews because their widows were being neglected in the daily distribution of food. And the twelve called together the whole community of disciples and said, "It is not right that we should neglect the word of God in order to wait on tables. Therefore, friends, select from among yourselves seven men of good standing, full of the Spirit and of wisdom, whom we may appoint to this task, while we, for our part, will devote ourselves to prayer and to serving the word." What they said pleased the whole community, and they chose Stephen, a man full of faith and the Holy Spirit, together with Philip, Prochorus, Nicanor, Timon, Parmenas, and Nicolaus, a proselyte of Antioch. They

> had these men stand before the apostles, who prayed and laid their hands on them. (Acts 6:1–6)

Healthcare, social service, and care of widows and orphans expanded the job description.

Then Paul's missionary adventures came along and a communal meeting space was vital for the cohesion and safety of those who followed. Eventually that changed from a catacomb to a house church to a clapboard meetinghouse, or ornate cathedral. And as things would have it, church leaders with families realized that they needed compensation for overseeing the multiple tasks of their ministry. With that realization, the job expanded to include administrative concerns: fundraising and building maintenance were added to the "to do" list. If we peruse the challenging, fulfilling, yet daunting jack-of-all-trades list, we might consider what public-sector jobs match up to the professional skills that are called into service in parish ministry:

- public speaker
- weekly-event planner
- scholar
- educator
- therapist
- writer and author
- healer
- social service professional
- social-event planner
- fundraiser
- human resources manager
- research librarian
- community leader
- manual laborer

- crisis intervention consultant
- missionary

I could add: studying a biblical text in a Greek language that is no longer spoken; counseling with a person who is spiritually struggling while facing illness and doesn't understand the nuances of the healthcare system; coordinating the human resources, volunteer and paid, in carrying out extensive organizational programs; mastering public relations and outreach; hammering nails with youth on a mission trip—the activities and skills required are overwhelming.

Some parishioners may be looking for Jesus, but the reality is that what they are seeking is a jack-of-all-trades. That sixteenth-century English phrase was originally a term of honor. It referred to workers who were multifaceted (multitasking) in their abilities. It was not until the seventeenth century that "master of none" was added.[1] An important part of clergy education is to broaden the skills base of the parish leader. Continuing education of church leaders should include courses and immersion experiences in what some would call secular professional fields of study. On several occasions I have taken courses at the American Management Association in a variety of topics and fields. Along with the joy that comes with learning something new and developing broader skills, I also learned about the psyches and spiritual journeys of business professionals in those areas of work. While all who lead in a parish bring their own particular gifts to their ministries, a broadening of these abilities is essential for effective leadership. This is particularly important for those serving in smaller church settings where having professional staff colleagues is usually not possible. Being Jesus is out of the question. Being an effective communicator of Christ's message increasingly requires a jack-of-all-trades leadership style.

In addition to the broad range of skills needed for dynamic church leadership, there are also key roles that are at the heart of vital ministry. These roles play themselves out through all of the ministerial activities. While they may have been interwoven into the designation of pastor and teacher, we need a fresh look at the roles that are the catalyst for a healthy church. A refreshed list might include these seven:

1. cheerleader
2. gift consultant
3. comforter of the afflicted and afflicter of the comfortable
4. question raiser
5. travel agent
6. teacher of alien education
7. purveyor of blessings

1. Cheerleader

It's no accident that, early on in his preaching Jesus proclaimed to a mostly ragtag group of inquisitive souls and committed followers, "You are the salt of the earth" and "You are the light of the world." It is also no accident that the advertising industry subtly tries to tell us that we are incomplete and insufficient, and we need this cosmetic or this shirt or this exercise sneaker or this car or this pill or this diet plan or this credit card—the list is endless—to feel good about ourselves and know in our souls that we are worthy of being loved. Ronald Rolheiser in his book *Against an Infinite Horizon,* writes that the Jesuit priest Karl Rahner caught the essence of this spiritual incompleteness when he wrote in a spiritual reflection about "the torment of insufficiency" being woven into the fabric of our being.[2] There is an uneasiness inside of us that we are insufficient! We all seek a little affirmation of our goodness and wholeness and a timely word that life is good and hope is ours in abundance. The image of cheerleader fits this role. It is the cheerleaders who make the players on the team feel positive and hopeful. It is the cheerleaders who shout: "Never give up. We'll win in the end!" The church is the place where we're to be told in word and deed that we are the light of the world and that "in hope we were saved. Now hope that is seen is not hope. For who hopes for what is seen? But if we hope for what we do not see, we wait for it with patience" (Rom 8:24–25). Ours is a ministry of encouragement, of whispering or shouting when needed to those to whom we minister. "You are the light of the world!" In Christ you are sufficient and whole!

2. Gift Consultant

"Now there are varieties of gifts, but the same Spirit; and there are varieties of services, but the same Lord; and there are varieties of activities, but it is the same God who activates all of them in everyone. To each is given the manifestation of the Spirit for the common good" (1 Cor 12:4–7). This is the foundation on which our gift-consulting ministry is based. This role requires attentive listening and active inquiry into the lives of the members of the congregation. By its very nature the church should be a safe haven where people can test their gifts without judgment. The church should be a place that needs the employment of all if lay persons' gifts if its ministry is to be faithful and effective. Gift identification and deployment is a core role to be played by those who seek to build up the Body of Christ.

3. Comforter of the Afflicted and Afflicter of the Comfortable

In the early twentieth century, the Chicago humorist Finley Peter Dunne said the role of the newspaper is to "Comfort the afflicted and afflict the comfortable."[3] This quote is often linked to the role of clergy. It is an apt pastoral function. Again there is no better model than Jesus. He would lift up the downtrodden and bring down the high and mighty. He would comfort the broken in body and spirit and would pry open the eyes of those who were blinded to their self-righteousness by their pride-swollen faces. The church is the place where for the individual and common good love is given to the brokenhearted. And it is there that truth in love is spoken to the hard-hearted. This ministry requires prayerful discernment so that the word of healing is clearly heard and the word of judgment is graciously shared with candor.

3. Question Raiser

My father taught me that discerning and thoughtful questions can lead to profound insights. “Is that right?” “Is that the faithful thing to do?” “What do you think?” “What do you see and hear?” “How do you think that person feels?” In the Gospel of Matthew alone Jesus asks at least eighty-seven questions. Jesus believed questions lead to deep spiritual insight. Good questions lead to many obvious answers about relationships and life—often answers that we would prefer not to address because they require us to change our presuppositions or behaviors. You get the feeling that Jesus is saying, “I ask the question, but deep inside you really know the answer.” Those who lead must be sensitive in shaping the questions and must be humble enough to admit to those who are questioned that they are also on the journey. Only when we are seeking the answer together will the Spirit offer the wisdom needed to answer the question. Church leadership should remind us that a prayerfully shaped question can be more life changing than an offering of shallow platitudes and easy answers.

4. Travel Agent

The reality for a large majority of us is that we live with a limited worldview. Even with twenty-four-hour news cycles and technology that opens the world to us, we are globally challenged creatures. We live the majority of our lives within a limited physical and cultural geography. The groups with which we affiliate usually have as the bonding agent some common elements: family lifestyles, level of education and professional expertise, political affiliation, socioeconomic status, avocational interests. We rarely travel outside our time zone or comfort zone and are limited in our knowledge of people with different cultural, geographic, or socioeconomic backgrounds. All of our travels do little to break down our provincial worldviews. We have voluminous pictures of the sights we have seen but have little insight into the soul of the places we have been and the souls of the people who live in those places. The stories from my ministry are vast when it comes to the limited worldview of the majority. For almost a decade and a half of my ministry I lived outside of Hartford, Connecticut. Hartford was and still is one of the poorest cities in the nation. A major east-west road, Route 44, runs through one of the most impoverished and blight-ravaged sections of the city. On one occasion I was commenting about travel time to a community on the other side of Hartford. The person who also drove to that town was fascinated that my travel time was considrably less than his. I drove through that greatly neglected section of Hartford, not around it. It seems my friend was willing to take fifteen minutes longer on his trip to avoid "that section" of the city. I could not help but engage him in a conversation about "those people" who lived in "that section." There were José and María, the owners of a bodega that served the best jerk chicken in town. There was the library night watchman, Charles, and his wife, Mildred, who worked as a hotel maid, and their three children. And there was Charlotte, a single mother who had been abandoned by her husband. She held down two part-time jobs while her mother cared for her two small children. She was proud that she and her children never missed church on Sunday mornings. Yes, there were the drug dealers in the projects and the supposed "work for food" con artists. But the great majority of "those people" were women and men with the same human emotions and dreams as those who wanted to avoid "that part of the city." My friend was amazed at my revelations.

Whether it's Paul's challenge to break down the dividing walls or Jesus' encounter with the "different" and rejected Samaritan woman at Jacob's Well (Jn 4), the church is called to be the place that expands the worldview of its members. And the pastor is called to be the primary travel planner and coordinator. In our ever-emerging global village the church needs to embrace the challenge of tearing down the walls. It needs to draw people away from their spiritual, cultural, and geographic comfort zones. The development of settings where people of different faith perspectives, cultural backgrounds, racial hues, sexual preferences, and any other dividing criteria come together needs to be a foundational element in the church's program ministry. When the pastor or core church leadership takes on this role of travel agent, they are being faithful to Christ's call to go to all the world.

5. Teacher of Alien Education

In their provocative classic book *Resident Aliens,* Stanley Hauerwas and William H. Willimon put forward the idea that the purpose of the church is not to foster a mind-set of helping people to fit into the world in which they live, but rather to become a place where resident aliens of this world can be supported and reminded of the values of the other world which, through faith, they inhabit.[4] We are called not to be conformed to this world, but to be spiritually transformed so that we may boldly remain aliens in this world. The church leader is called to present again and again the fruits of the Spirit that are the basis for living in the world but not of it, to quote Paul. The leader is to constantly remind the community that we live our lives by a different set of values that keep us alert to the seductive nature of the world's values. The body building trainer and leader must ask the difficult and, to some, annoying question "Are we living by God's standards or the world's?" When spiritually emboldened, I have asked this question at church leadership meetings: the Bible, our guide to living an abundant life, teaches much about what is out of sync and in direct conflict with this world's values and behavior patterns. Unless we are consistently reminded of the principles of alien education and unless we have a supportive community in which alien behaviors are modeled and cherished, it is easy to allow the operational principles of this world to capture our hearts. Once when I was asked the function of the sermon, I responded, "It's to remind us weekly what it means to be an alien in this world." Dynamic church leaders are teachers of alien education.

6. Purveyor of Blessings

Again it is the Oblate priest, writer, and spiritual retreat leader Ronald Rolheiser who helps to clarify our role as purveyor of blessings when he reflects on the human cry to be blessed and the meaning of a blessing.

> The word "blessing" takes its root from the Latin verb *benedicere,* to speak well of (*bene* well, *dicere* to speak). Therefore to bless someone is, through some word, gesture, or ritual, to

> make that person aware of three things: (1) the goodness of the original creation where, after making the earth and humans, God said that it was "good, very good"; (2) that God experiences the same delight and pleasure in him or her that God experienced with Jesus at his baptism when he said: "This is my beloved child in whom I take delight"; and (3) that we, who are giving the blessing, recognize that goodness and take delight in the other person.[5]

The body building leader offers blessings in abundance.

I was fortunate to see the purveying of blessings modeled out in a beloved colleague who led a national office of the United Church of Christ in which I worked for several years. All who were touched by his ministry considered the Reverend Doctor Ruben Sheares a beloved and respected national leader. It was his practice at some point in a conversation (always spontaneously) to say to the other person, "Well, bless your heart!" His presence reflected a bright light because he was a purveyor of blessings. The word "purveyor" is appropriate because it implies one who brings food and clothing to journeyers, often in wilderness, pioneering settings. The body building leader is to bring the sustenance of the Spirit and the armor of God to the faith-journeying traveler.

The multiple roles we are called to assume in our professional lives seem overwhelming! While pastors and other Christian leaders are not to be Jesus, they are called to represent Jesus. They should be jacks-of-all-trades in their expansive ministry roles. Ministry requires one more challenging role: Did you ever consider being a juggler? This is actually implicit in any job description for a person who is called to minister in a parish setting.

Inspiration

It should be our hope that our ministry will lead others to proclaim:

> When it's over, I want to say all my life
> I was a bride married to amazement.
> I was the bridegroom, taking the world into my arms.
>
> —Mary Oliver[6]

Prayer

Okay, God, you who supposedly equip and call your people to ministry, I need to be honest with you in that I'm not sure I'm equipped to be a jack-of-all-trades. My skills are limited and my character is sometimes a little frayed. I guess all I'm asking for is your help in using me to show your grace, even when I am less than perfect in responding to the calls that ministry will bring. Amen.

3

How Many Balls Can You Juggle?

Insights into Getting the Job Done without Losing Your Mind or Spirit

Body Building Exercises

- What do you believe people would say are the top three job priorities of clergy?
- What are the parts of ministry that you like the best? What are the parts of ministry that you like the least?
- How would you define your organizational and management style?

Anthony Gallo can only juggle nine balls, and only for fifty-four seconds. As church leaders seeking to be effective and faithful in building up the Body of Christ, this is something we need to remember. "Who is Anthony Gallo?" you might ask. He is a record-setting professional juggler. One of his records is juggling nine balls for a mere fifty-four seconds.[1] His accomplishment proves it is impossible to juggle very many things for any great length of time. It's almost hopeless to pay attention to nine things at once, and it's physically and mentally draining to keep too many balls in the air.

The reality of our role as jugglers became apparent to me in one tragic moment. It was a moment when those multiple calls challenged my spiritual and physical strength. During the Easter season over a two-week period, I faced the writing of three sermons, preparing and leading four Bible studies, attending three church leadership meetings, assisting in the oversight of four youth group meetings, officiating at one wedding, finishing newsletter material, being pleasant during dozens of drop-in visits to my office, attending two town meetings, making customary hospital calls, counseling with two families in crisis—oh, and, yes, overseeing the pastoral and liturgical needs for four funerals involving eight people. Of those four funerals, one involved a tragically incomprehensible car accident in which two grandparents had died, leaving two other people in comas. While I tried to implement the best organizational and time management possible, it ended up as a two-week, 24/7 roller-coaster ride.

While this two-week period is far from the norm, a church leader's week can easily turn chaotic. It's impossible to schedule for the drop-in visit of a parishioner who has a personal concern and just needs someone to listen, or the health-related crisis call that demands immediate attention, or the call from a family or funeral home asking for a compassionate presence *now*. The yearnings and idiosyncrasies of the human spirit do not easily fit into prefixed time slots. The reality is that the interruptions are often the most important parts of Christian ministry.

Christian leaders have been and always will be expected to multitask. Many of us wear that designation as a badge of honor. If we are honest with ourselves and if we believe the current research on multitasking, such an operational style is actually less than effective in getting the job done correctly. There is a very insightful definition of multitasking: "Multitasking is the act of messing up several things at once." Multitasking may have worked when it meant the parallel-processing abilities of computers, but it isn't very effective when put into the hands of humans. The rapid development of communications technology has created heightened expectations for instant feedback and has been a catalyst for increased multitasking. Whether we are in the office or at the dinner table, our ability to give our fullest attention to one person or one task is constantly being compromised by the interruptions that undisciplined technology causes. The psychologist René Marois of Vanderbilt University found that multitasking is actually a very ineffective tool for getting the job done correctly. "Marois found evidence of a 'response selection bottleneck' that occurs when the brain is forced to respond to several stimuli at once. As a result, task switching leads to time lost as the brain determines which task to perform."[2] If multitasking leads to inefficiency and less than excellence in performance, then how are we as church leaders to accomplish graciously and competently the many calls on our time and attention? There are at least three preliminary steps we must take:

1. Knowing Ourselves

Managing the many tasks of ministry begins long before the call to a local church. It starts with an honest and thoughtful reflection on the leader's skills and talents, as well as professional weaknesses. Part of the discernment process before ordination, as well as at times of transition in ministry, needs to include an honest assessment of "Who am I?" and "What are my strengths and weaknesses?" There may be a heightened expectation to ask these questions particularly at times of personal or organizational conflict. Some denominations and seminaries require psychological and vocational testing before one can enter the ordained ministry.

It will be difficult to forget a week-long intensive group program at seminary prior to the beginning of the formal academic year. The "T-Group" experience brought together a dozen second-year seminary students for the purpose of fostering introspection. A trainer managed the group interaction. For eight hours a day we were sequestered in a classroom with the only agenda being to talk about each individual and how others perceived us. One student was so slow paced in his dealing with life that he received this less than loving feedback: "You move like a turtle, and it takes you half an hour to get out of your mouth any worthwhile thought!" The student's response was: "It's just my nature!" To which came the retort: "If you can't change your nature, some local church will send you back to nature." Because of my efforts to be positive and come across as an average all-American guy, I received a "You remind me of a goddamned Norman Rockwell painting! You need to get *dirtied up!*" At first the group process seemed excruciatingly painful. However, by the end of the week's session most of the participants were greatly enlightened as to how others perceived them and had a deeper understanding of their leadership strengths and weaknesses. It might be a healthy practice to select loving parishioners and spiritual mentors whom we ask periodically to give us honest feedback. Self-knowledge can empower us to lead.

2. Getting the Expectations Clear before Accepting a Call

There is another discernment that needs to take place prior to accepting a call to a local church. The expectations of the calling church's priorities need to be discussed with full candor. "How many balls are they expecting me to juggle?" During the interview and call process, time must be taken to ascertain whether skills match up with the church's ministerial leadership expectations. Often candidates for a position do not fully grasp the complete "work" expectations of the membership. Candidates should be encouraged to ask questions that dig beneath the platitudes about ministry expectations, such as: "What are the three top priorities on which I should spend my time?" When considering a call, it can be helpful to turn the tables on the search committee by setting up a case study concerning a day when a multitude of church concerns collide with family obligations. With the case study before them, the question could be offered: "With the needs of family requiring my attention, how would you prioritize my ministry tasks?" This pre-call discernment helps to clarify how many balls the church membership expects its leader to juggle.

3. Gaining Insights on Skillful Juggling

Compared with many other professions, parish leadership has numerous unique characteristics. During a sabbatical leave I enrolled in a course at the American Management Association in New York City. It was a course for upper-level managers. I felt it would be helpful to me since I had just shifted roles at the church from associate to senior minister. Now with primary responsibility for the administrative oversight of the church it seemed a wise continuing education decision. At the end of the two-week course I was asked by a CEO of a medium-sized corporation what I had learned. I confided in him that I appreciated much of the organizational oversight information but was having a difficult time making a clear connection between what I learned and my role as a leader (COO) of a church. Upon receiving his encouragement I offered an honest thought that caught his attention: “In my place of employment, the shareholders, who invest their time, talent, and treasure in the company, are also the workers. You can fire a worker for not doing the job you expect, but I cannot fire a (volunteer) shareholder.” While an effective pastor or leader must make some assumptions about authority given to him or her, the job performance expectations are constantly being redefined by individual members (shareholders) of the church. To make matters more difficult, when the church COO, the pastor, assigns tasks to the volunteer workers and they fail to complete their task sadequately, firing is not an option; compassionate diplomacy is. Along with the expansiveness of the leadership roles, this reality requires some basic instruction in the art of juggling.

An instructional guide for the pastor/juggler might include the following:

- Prioritizing—Some things are more important than others
- Organizing—Create systems that help in the art of juggling
- Healing—We must let go of the Elijah Complex

Prioritizing

There are people to marry and bury; there are pastoral calls to make; there’s a Sunday worship service with a sermon plan; there’s church school curriculum to help select or write; there are wider church meetings to attend; there’s a disgruntled choir member to listen to; there’s a newsletter article to write; there’s confirmation class to teach; there’s a building and grounds concern that is suddenly crucial; there’s prayer group and Bible study to lead and attend; there’s . . . ! So many things to accomplish and so little time! Unless the leader develops priorities, chaos will ensue and all the balls will fall to the ground. My priority has always been pastoral care. It is a ministry that the human soul longs for and it’s the ministry that builds the trust required for a healthy Body of Christ. When pastoral care is effective many of the other ministry roles can be implemented without interference or conflict. Where there is trust, support for creativity and innovation will follow. Others might disagree, but the worship service runs a close second on the priority list. The most public of responsibilities, services must be well developed and dramatically presented. Regardless of the ordering, prioritization is essential. Having a prioritized list established can provide the filter to avoid having too many balls airborne at once.

Organizing

There are thousands of books and articles on time management, yet a distillation of the plethora of material as it relates to parish ministry is rare.

Early on in one's ministry the organization of time and space and the use of resources need to be established. Almost every time management resource encourages the concept of time blocks. Designation of blocks of time for the varying ministry activities is indispensable. Having portions of the day assigned to particular tasks gives focus to ministry. Even assigning uncommitted time blocks gives structure to the day. While important interruptions will occur, an unscheduled ministry leads to a chaotic ministry designed by the interruptions. Depending on body clocks, family lifestyles, and the priorities of a particular church's ministry, the blocking of time will vary. I personally encourage that at least two time blocks be permanent parts of a pastor's schedule: a time for personal Bible study, intercessory prayer, and meditation, and a time for family interaction. These times keep us grounded and alert. The establishment of a time block system helps bring focus to the task at hand. It allows us to proficiently concentrate on just one ball at a time. To strengthen this organizational style, a wide range of print and online time management resources are available.

Living in our communication-overloaded society also requires time management for responding to the increasing number of technology-related interruptions. For several years I have lived in the world of Android communication. My phone has a groaning D-r-o-i-d which reminds me every few minutes of a new e-mail, text, voice mail, or news release. It became my foolish and often insensitive habit to instantaneously respond to the communications whenever they arrived. My cell owned me; I didn't own it. It became obvious to others that I wasn't really present with them because I was paying attention to the rings and groans of cellular technology. Several time blocks scattered throughout our daily schedule for responding to the frequent technology-related contacts brings focus to all the other calls for our attention.

Other distractions are close at hand: "Now let's see, where did I file that sermon illustration on forgiveness? Did I put it under 'S' for sermon or 'F' for forgiveness? Is it in the pile of papers on my desk or on the bookshelf? Maybe I cut and pasted it into one of my computer files. Is it on drive C, or on the desktop, or maybe I put it on the blue flash drive?" There is truth to the old joke: What is a filing system? A place where things get alphabetically lost. More time is wasted than we could ever imagine in the search for that information or document or file. Whether it is desk space or cyberspace, a manageable space plan is foundational to avoiding considerable wasted time.

Two small signs adorn my desk. One reads "A cluttered desk, a mark of a genius." The other reads "If a cluttered desk is a sign of a cluttered mind, what is an empty desk?" Although my desk may look messy, anyone who has ever known me can vouch that I know where everything is on it. It may look cluttered, but it's organized. Regardless of first appearances, each space on my desk and around my bookcases is categorized. Yes, there has been the rare time when I made a frantic call to my administrative assistant in search of some document or information. But in spite of personal preferences in organizational style, in order to juggle effectively, a space-use pattern needs to be established. For those who have the gift of competent support staff, the organizing task is made easier. Most church leaders, however, are not afforded this luxury. A good assessment tool of whether we are organized or not is the "Can I find it in five minutes?" test. Indeed, God created an orderly universe! The challenge is our ability to create order in a much smaller universe called our office.

In our organizational planning, we are fortunate to have the gift of microchip technology to give us a leg up on those who came before us. The selection of resources to support effective and efficient juggling requires objective and even prayerful study. Particularly with the ever increasing marketplace of computer hardware and software, decisions about the purchase of support hardware and software can be complicated. This should be guided by personal competencies with the technology, the learning-curve time required, configuration of church staff, and the networking capabilities of the resource. In most church settings, the up-front costs and long-term associated expenses for upkeep and maintenance are significant factors to consider. The multiuse capabilities of the hardware and the availability of church-friendly software are important considerations. The nuances in resource selection became evidently clear to me in a discussion I had with my reference-librarian wife. We were talking about different search engines. I am tied to Google. She's a Bing fan. In an effort to help me manage my time she highlighted the fact that Bing gives a better synopsis of search results, gaining time while reducing efforts to gather research. While I'll continue to stubbornly use Google, it reaffirmed that care needs to be taken beforehand when organizing for effective digital support in the local church.

When organizing, we need to address our ADOS (Attention Deficit Organization System). Underlying much of our preaching is the message that in an AD society we have to pay attention if we want to experience the presence of God. In a world of multiple options, where the iPad had four releases of new hardware in one year, and where new apps are available daily, we have a tendency to activate the ADOS gene in all of us. We just have to have the latest this or that. An increasing number of people are constantly changing their operational styles and equipment because there's a new tech toy or gadget available. The visual parable of our time is waiting lines every six months outside Apple stores when the latest phone or tablet is being released. Most churches have members in their community who are always suggesting changing to the newest software. There's a seductive, even a status, factor about owning the newest gadget. A minimum of a three-year life cycle on time, space, and resource components should be strongly considered. This avoids the time wasting that comes with continual evaluation and constant change. One of the biggest time wasters can be the learning curve when incorporating new technology in the ministry.

A key component in the final implementation of becoming a talented juggler is the education of church leaders and the congregation about the multiple calls for your attention and letting people know the broad outlines of your schedule. Unless we let the community of faith know what we do with our time, "you only work on Sundays" will be the understanding by which some will view our ministry. Having a well-defined, broadly published schedule is not only an organization strategy but an educational tool. It can never hurt to occasionally review weekly schedules in leadership meetings so that leaders know the scope and scale of our ministries and can give guidance to and support for our juggling of the many balls of parish ministry.

The calls for our attention will be multitudinous. Unless we set priorities and establish well-defined organizational systems, then, as an insightful pastor said, "We will tend toward becoming a quivering mass of availability."

Healing

A relevant scripture passage for dealing with juggling is found in Elijah's powerful encounter with God on the top of Mt. Horeb. As you will recall, he's running scared from King Ahab and his revengeful wife, Jezebel. He has destroyed the prophets of Baal. As he meditates, seeking God's comfort and wisdom, he tells God—twice, mind you—"I alone am left!" Translation: "I am the only one left who can responsibly carry the message of your goodness! Holy One, I am it, and I'll have to do it alone if it's to get done right!" There is a propensity for church leaders to take on the Elijah complex: "No one else can do it as well as I can and, even if they have the best intentions, they just can't do it right. I have to juggle all this alone!" Often such a complex leads to a negativity that will undermine our ministry.

Without a doubt the most effective tool for juggling is the realization that there are others who can help. There are other faithful souls who can join us. They have gifts and talents that enable them to partner with us to spread the Good News. Along with doing our ministry, we are called to equip the saints to do their ministry.

If we believe Paul's teaching, that there are many gifts but one Spirit, then it is our responsibility to identify these gifts and talents. Using an extra copy of a church directory to identify and list the talents of each church member is time well spent. In the building of powerful lay ministry, several considerations are worth heeding:

- Would members' abilities to serve be based on a love of church or a need to be needed?
- Can they work well with others?
- Are they spiritually grounded? Are they mature in their personality and faith?
- How much supervision or training will be required?
- Would they be more effective in a one-time or an ongoing ministry?

While it has been my privilege to serve only in multiplestaff churches I was also fortunate enough to have been a judicatory official with pastors of fifty small-membership churches. In most denominations, more than 60 percent of the churches have fewer than two hundred members. Along with my admiration for those who served in small-membership churches I was overwhelmed by their week-after-week preaching schedule. On two interim occasions when I was the sole minister, the challenges of weekly preaching became obvious and tedious. To remain fresh in the pulpit and to reclaim valuable time for the other calls for my attention, the solution was obvious: find others to preach occasionally. And why not the laity? The task of identifying articulate and committed lay preachers produced four members who answered the call. To insure meaningful preaching, brief training sessions were designed. Understanding liturgy, effective biblical exegesis, public speaking, and creative writing were the foci of the four-week training. The rewards of occasionally having the laity in the pulpit were threefold: (1) Many in the pews could relate to the unordained preacher's journey; (2) there was excitement from the lay preacher that in one case led to ordination; and (3) the pastor's calendar now had six to twelve hours a week free to attend to other ministry activities. Juggling as a team makes for energized ministry.

For those serving in settings where support and professional staff are available, sharing in the juggling of the many aspects of ministry is more easily accomplished. In a team setting, remember:

- Trusted and talented administrative assistants can ease the load and make you look better than you really are. They can help you organize, cover for you, and keep you honest and humble. So choose wisely!
- Your professional colleagues are your colleagues, not your subordinates. Keep in constant communication with them. Laugh and cry with them. Pray and play together. Avoid making them *gofers* and share the high-visibility ministries with them. If you do, they will cover your back.
- Advocate for your support staff (secretarial staff, property personnel, etc.) to be seen as full partners in ministry. Affirm their importance by offering frequent praise and advocating for fair work schedules and compensation. Do likewise for the professional staff.

While many clergy would deny it, one of the biggest challenges to multistaff ministry is jealousy among staff when praise is given. Praise given to one staff member should be seen as praise for the entire team. This should be the spirit nurtured by the leader. A staff with team members who have different personal and leadership styles is an asset. Such diversity allows a larger portion of the congregation to feel connected with the church.

Hidden within the deep recesses of the eclectic book from the Hebrew scriptures, Ecclesiastes, are the profound words "Two are better than one, because they have good reward for their toil." It continues by pointing out that companionship in doing a task brings physical and emotional strength to the work.

There is one area of togetherness that can help to alleviate some of the dropped balls of overextended juggling. It is often viewed with a jaundiced eye. That area of support is working with other churches.

Joining together in ministry with one or several other churches is difficult because while they are partners in Christ's ministry in a particular community, they are also competitors for members. That is a painfully honest truth. Such teamwork does require a level of transparent honesty among the participating churches' leaderships. The reality of competition needs to be openly discussed, and a balanced and truly shared leadership approach must be affirmed.

Other community groups and agencies are also resources for teamwork. If a nonreligious organization or agency is meeting a need, we must consider the redundancy of a program we might wish to implement. Redundancy in programming may add an unneeded ball to juggle.

In 2010, Alex Barron and David Leahy set a world record for juggling twenty balls. That's eleven more than Anthony Gallo was able to juggle alone.[3] The body building leader will increase her or his juggling proficiency when priorities are established, organizational structures are in place, and the Elijah complex is cured.

Inspiration

In his book *Teaching Your Children about God,* David Wolpe relates a story about a father and son walking and coming upon a large stone. The boy asks the father whether if he uses all his strength the boy will be able to move the stone. The boy tries but fails. The father reminds his son of an important truth: "You didn't use all your strength—you didn't ask me to help."[4]

Prayer

God, in the divine circus of life you have called me to be one of the jugglers of the many calls that ministry in your name requires. When the calls seem too overwhelming, remind me that group juggling is pleasing in your sight. Help me to keep my eyes on the essential calls so that they are done to your glory. But most importantly, fix my eyes on Jesus so my spiritual dexterity is nimble and I will be amazed at the feats of hope and healing we accomplish together. Amen.

4

"Hymn #440 Will Always Be Hymn #440, and That's Final!"

How Body Builders Help a Church Deal with Change, the Only Constant

Body Building Exercises

- What changes would you like to take place in the church that you serve?
- Have you ever experienced a time in your life when you found change difficult? When was it, and why was it difficult for you to change?
- What do you think are three keys to successful change that do not divide a church?

The old hymnals were in a near-death condition. The maroon covers were fading. The pages were fraying. And the corpus of hymns in them was getting smaller and smaller as a new generation of worshippers with their own musical tastes was arriving in the pews. There were no hymns written after 1956 in sight. Moreover, since the current hymnal would no longer be in print, rebinding over five hundred of them would be very expensive. In light of the ultimate demise of this musical tome, a hymnal committee was commissioned that reflected the diversity of the church. The task would not be an easy one because of the many options. Several ideas were dismissed quite quickly.

Since we were a United Church of Christ body, the ultraconservative theology of some hymnals was noted and they were passed by with respect. The option of using technology was considered. But since technology was in its infancy and installing pull-down screens and hiding projectors could not be aesthetically accomplished in a classic New England meetinghouse, this option, too, was passed by with respect. Finally, the committee selected three hymnals that would meet most of the criteria established as benchmarks for candidacy as an acceptable resource for singing our praise to God.

The committee held six open meetings for feedback purposes. Naturally, some familiar hymns were now found in different sections of the suggested hymnals and some changes in language had taken place. In one most memorable moment during the discussions and deliberations, one very traditionalist member of the church stood tall and firmly proclaimed: "Hymn #440 will always be hymn #440, and that's final." There were allusions and subtle innuendos by this member about leaving the church and taking some friends with her if a hymnal that suited her desires could not be found. As our discussions to select a new hymnal continued, it became obvious that the hymnal for many held equal esteem to the Bible itself. The less-than-subtle message was "We are not enthused about changing long-held traditions."

A truth that we all know is that change is the only thing constant in life. Growth is a part of life, and thus change is at the heart of being alive. Growth means change, and change involves risk, stepping from the known to the unknown. The Gospels speak about the inevitability of change and offer comfort amid the change with comforting news: "Do not worry about tomorrow" because the "God of hosts is with us." God's Spirit journeys with us; we have nothing to fear. Still, in a world where the rapidity of change is ever increasing, and where nothing seems to be tied down, people are looking for a place where things *are* tied down and the winds of change are not always buffeting them. For many, the place where they have historically looked for familiarity is the church.

Many people of faith have forgotten that through the prophet Isaiah God announced, "I am doing a new thing." Through the parable of the old and new wineskins, Jesus proclaimed that faith is a process of continual fermentation. Protestant Christians tend to forget that it was through the change agent-act of the Reformation that we were given birth. The reality is that while the core beliefs of our faith are changeless, there are always going to be new ways for new days so that the Good News remains relevant in every age. The United Church of Christ, the denomination that has nurtured my faith since birth and in which I serve, adopted a "God is still speaking" theme as a way of identifying its core faith values. The symbol of a comma used in the still-speaking logo says it all. With God there are no periods, only an announcement that God has more light to shine. That means change is woven into the fabric of creation.

So the question for church leaders becomes *How do we lead a church in a way that change is handled prayerfully, compassionately, and seriously, and so that change does not become a divisive factor, rather than strengthening the Body of Christ?*

Regardless of setting—business, family, church—there is a standard process that can avoid the derailment of the needed change and the divisiveness that can tear apart the community of faith. To some I may be stating the obvious, but failure to remember the pitfalls that can accompany change is always perilous.

- Discern the need. Often the need is obvious. The leak in the sanctuary ceiling is now dripping water onto the pews; the participation in worship or the number of children in the church school is in drastic decline. Then there are the less obvious calls for change that are more difficult to conceptualize: the spirit in the church has become cynical and negative; the neighborhood around the church is becoming more ethnically diverse. Often a formal process of writing a statement will help to identify the vision the church desires and the obvious changes needed to reach the goal imbedded in the statement. However, there are warnings that need to be heeded. The vision statement should be as specific as possible. Too many vision statements end up with dozens and dozens of prosaic literary efforts that sound grand and majestic, yet they have no basis in reality and offer no clarity of what will need to be done to attain the articulated vision. "First Church seeks to be a church that reflects the principles of the realm of God and offers the selfless love of Jesus Christ to all the world." Isn't this what every church wants to be? Are there two specific characteristics that could be emphasized? How about being a family church that cares for the poor in the local community? Above all, beware of statements that are filled with platitudes! Also remember, don't take an eternity to get the vision mission statement written. A reasonable goal should be four to six months from the beginning of the envisioning process to the presentation of the statement. A small cross-section committee of the congregation can accomplish this writing task with regular and effective meetings.

- *Build the coalition.* In the leadership role as dream interpreter, we should be persistently alert for individuals who appear to have common hopes and dreams for the future of their church. We need to ascertain the size of the coalition that can be built to carry the dream to fruition. The respect and power of the people sharing a dream and their passion to implement the dream need to be considered. We also need to pay heed to the gravitas of those who might oppose the initiative. In our leadership role we're the ones to filter the dreams and decide which of them should be given priority. We then build the coalition and join it. It does not become "mine" but "ours." We lead by assisting those with the passion for the dream in the sometimes circuitous route to fulfillment. Rarely should we go it alone.
- *Write a plan that can stand up to serious and foolish scrutiny, presenting the plan in a positive and compelling way, and avoiding "uh . . ." and dull moments.* Avoid going public before a thoroughly researched, clearly written plan for fulfilling the dream is in place that answers:
  - What are the biblical and faith foundations that give validity and vitality to the plan?
  - What are the realities and needs that led to the goal in the plan?
  - How will the plan benefit the ministry of the church? What are the exact details of what the implemented plan will look like in the way of programs and personnel?

- What resources, including financial, will be required to reach the goal?
- What is the timeline to reach the goal? In preparing the details of the plan, the most important task to be accomplished by a coalition of the passionate and committed is to raise and answer the most difficult questions that could be asked by others. Not everyone will be easily convinced.

◆ *Never go public until all of what might be the toughest questions that could be asked have been answered.* It is extremely helpful to prepare a document with these and other questions, and use the answers as a script for those who will present the plan. It also can be an invaluable tool for inclusion in any materials to be shared with the church membership. "Uh . . ." moments when a question about the dream and its implementation cannot be answered do not help to garner support from the congregation.

◆ *Sell the plan with effective marketing.* It needs to be sold in a positive and upbeat manner. The selection of those who will be the visible face of the dream needs to be handled with the utmost care. Being faith-grounded, personable, articulate, able to think quickly on their feet, and respected by the majority of the congregation—these are the criteria for those who speak for the dream. A lifeless, lackluster presenter can lead to the death of some very worthy and needed initiatives. The roles of the devoted committee members need to be clearly defined through an open, honest, and prayerful reflection on the gifts of each individual participant in the group.

◆ *Distill the dream into a few concise, fervent, yet defining terms.* This is essential. Whether it's simply a small but significant change in church programming or a major capital campaign venture, a moniker that is descriptive and memorable is beneficial in building a supportive base. Creativity and imagination should reign in the development of this moniker or catchphrase. In an increasingly sound-bite-oriented society, a few well-chosen, pithy words that coalesce the goals of the vision will expand support for it. Often faith-based acronyms enhance the effort.

- *Share the plan with the appropriate audiences and don't take feedback or criticism personally.* It is important to recognize which people or groups will be most affected by the change. It may be a few individuals, a small group, a ministry area, or even the whole church. Our sensitivity to the concerns of these individuals and groups through soliciting their insights and suggestions can broaden support. Naturally, many forms of communication need to be used to engage the selected audiences. Along with face-to-face dialogue, mass communications and social networking should be considered as feedback tools. During this time of obtaining feedback, the pastor or leader may receive comments that allude to perceived deficiencies in his or her ministry. Don't take it personally, and make certain your own advocates are part of the public face of the feedback gathering. It is best that any defense of the ministry comes from the leadership of those who are ardent in support of the change rather than from the pastor or leader. Attentive listening, a thank you for feedback that will be considered, and, if needed, a contact from the pastor later are the most positive forms of response to any critique.
- *Move on through consensus with as few formal votes as possible.* While the vote is a cherished gift in our democratic society, taking votes in church except on the most significant issues is often unproductive. Seeking a consensus is a more appropriate way of dealing with change in the church because:
    - It requires honest and open dialogue rather than just showing up and casting a vote, and dialogue requires attentive listening that seeks to put the heart of Christ into the discussion.
    - Faith questions can be raised and discussed.
    - It opens the possibility of enhancing the suggested change, new initiatives, or plan so ownership by all can be more fully accepted.

- It helps to significantly avoid political coalition building and voting blocks that might suddenly appear at meetings where votes will be taken.
- It softens the less-than-faith-based concept of having winners and losers that can often accompany the taking a formal vote.
- It allows for identifying individuals who may need a pastoral presence after decisions have been made.
- It lessens the feeling of gravity of the change.

Naturally such a consensus process requires skilled moderating, as well as attentive listening. Transcribing the insights in a manner that all can see them strengthens the feeling of being heard. In some situations, congregational votes will need to be taken, but almost always consensus building is a more effective process for unifying the church in times of change.

How to Deal with Difficult People— And That's Final!

There will always be "hymn #440, and that's final" people on the scene along the way in ministry, particularly at times when changes are taking place within *my* church. Difficult, cantankerous, argumentative, grumpy . . . think of one of these people in your parish and add other adjectives to the list. Disruptive journeyers will come our way as we are traveling toward the Promised Land.

As they did with Moses, the disgruntled will complain and be bull-headed. A humorist once tried to help define a difficult person: "You're a difficult person if telemarketers hang up on you . . . you have to stand on your head to smile . . . your parents move and leave no forwarding address . . . people keep sending your obituary to the paper . . . there is a collective groan when you enter a meeting." Contrarian souls can weigh us down, impede the speed of the journey to the Promised Land, and deflate the morale of the community of faith. It is a reality, but not a good thing, to have negative voices gaining significant visibility in the life of any church.

Since their presence is invitable, how can we minimize their effect on the ministry of the church? While there are dozens of books and hundreds of websites on dealing with difficult people, few come from a faith perspective. With faith guiding our ministry we cannot write off or demonize the naysayers because we are commanded to love them. What are the best ways for dealing with difficult people?

- *Pastor, yes! Adversary, no!* Most people who are recalcitrant often have stories to tell about stress and feeling powerless. The church is supposed to be a welcoming place for broken souls, and often difficult people are the most in need of the embracing love and acceptance that the church offers. Therefore, time is needed to listen to the person's life story, as well as to his or her opinion. We begin with loving respect. Patience will be essential so the story can be decoded amid the opinions offered.
- *Stay positive! Don't join the argument*! "Let no evil talk come out of your mouths, but only what is helpful for building up, as there is need, so that your words may give grace to those who hear" (Eph 4:29). Keep down the volume. "You must understand this, my beloved: let everyone be quick to listen, slow to speak, slow to anger; for your anger does not produce God's righteousness" (James 1:19–20). Enough said!
- *Ask questions that appeal to reason and faith.* "Since a significant majority of the church believes in what we want to accomplish, where do you see the flaws in their thinking and in their way of accomplishing the task?" "While the dream may seem irrational, in looking at scripture, is it the faithful thing to do?" Often the difficult soul is responding emotionally to the issue at hand; reason and faith are needed in the discussion.
- *Mine the best of what is being offered; take any wisdom that may be in the contrarian opinion.* "Since many in the church feel the issue needs to be addressed, short of doing nothing, how would you address the need? What advice would you give to those implementing the goal?" This form of approach underscores that the majority rules but the thoughts of those who don't agree are important for the most positive outcome.

- *Use scripture and prayer as stress alleviators.* Asking the person for their favorite Bible passages and reading one of them, or opening the Bible and asking the person to read a selected verse sets a tone for the discussion. It can bring a difficult moment into perspective. Beginning the meeting with a prayer, calling for an open heart and mind, and asking that the time together be a moment of discernment of God's will can direct the tone of the discussion.
- *Love them but be clear you don't necessarily agree with their position or way of handling the difference of opinion.* We are called to love everyone even though we may not approve of their behavior. The mantra must be I love you . . . but I can't agree with you. This approach mixes compassion with firmness. Avoid attacking the person; it's the issue that needs to be addressed.
- *When all else fails, beseech the elders.* In the early church, extremely difficult people were dealt with through confrontation by their peers. If professional pastoral leadership fails to soften the soul of the person, it's time to bring in the heavy hitters, the lay leadership of the church. The first line of attack can come from family and friends. The second can come from the elected leadership of the church. It is true that lay leaders wish to avoid a straight and direct approach, but in rare cases of repetitive negativity that is hurting the spirit of the congregation, they must act for the welfare of the church. Even the most drastic of actions—"Perhaps you need to find another church that would better suit your needs"—should be one of the options at their disposal. Regardless of a person's history in the church, generosity of financial giving ,and so on, the lay leaders will need to lead in addressing some painful, church-dividing situations.
- *Don't become so preoccupied with the negative that it diminishes the positive in the life of the church.* The best antidote for dealing with difficult people is building a joyous and hope-filled spirit within the whole community of faith. Regardless of one's negativity, a positive and Spirit-filled community of faith drowns out those who will be habitually negative. It will be clear to all that negativity goes nowhere in this place. So as local church leaders, let us be

pastorally attentive to the difficult ones, but never let them distract us from leading our churches closer to the Promised Land.

Call it the early Christian church, call it the Protestant Reformation, call it the Great Awakening, call it Vatican II, or call it the emergent church movement—the church has survived and flourished because it has changed to adapt the old, old Gospel to the new social realities and contexts in which it has found itself. Remember this: at one time hymn #440 never existed. Remember that in the future it just might be hymn #276. Let us sing our praises to an unchanging God in an ever-changing world!

Inspiration

"In Pioneer Theology the church is the wagon train. It is always on the move. . . . [It] is not comfortable or safe. . . . [It] does not hesitate to move into the new. . . . The pioneers gladly trade safety for obedience to the insistent [voice of God]." —Wes Seeliger[1]

Prayer

God, your love for us never changes. Yet we realize that the only constant in life is change. Grant us the grace to be patient when others want to fight changes that will bring new life to the churches we serve. Give us the gift of divine discernment so that we will be able to separate what needs to be changed from what should remain changeless. We pray this in the name of the One who altered the course of history through his sacrificial life. Amen.

5

A Landmark, Not a Church—Really?

Geography and History Lessons: Body Building Leaders Make Them a Priority

Body Building Exercises

- What do nonmembers know about the church in which you are a member or which you are serving?
- What are the five most important historical events in the life of your church? Why are they important?
- If you were a parishioner in your church, what three things would you like the pastor to know about you? Why?

"What," I asked, "do you know about the church on the hill near the center of town?" I heard an assortment of answers.

"Oh, you mean that stone church on Boston Post Road? Why, that church is a town landmark! Sailors on Long Island Sound use its steeple to set their course back to shore."

"It's the church with the crocuses on the hill."

"Don't know much about the church. Sitting up on that hill it seems kind of distant. Its severe Gothic stone facade makes it look cold and foreboding!"

Then I asked, "Have you ever been inside the church or worshipped there?" The answer was usually "No!" A few mentioned they'd been inside for a wedding or a funeral. Another few of those questioned knew someone who was a member but knew nothing else about the church.

These were a few of the answers given to me by fifty random people when I, acting as if I were a stranger in town, walked the streets of Greenwich, Connecticut. Either before the call process, but always at the beginning of a ministry in a new church setting, it is advantageous to take “The Stranger in Town Survey.” Knowing early on in one’s ministry the physical and spiritual geography of a parish is one essential element for leadership that is invigorating and transformational. It is also a beneficial activity to carry out on a periodic basis as a way of evaluating any changes in perceptions of the church.

It is an often overlooked truth that all churches are not alike. One size does not fit all. In the churches I have served or consulted with, the membership numbers have varied greatly: 39, 110, 350, 735, 1143, 1878. They have been in city, suburban, and rural settings. The demographic makeup of these churches has included hard-working farmers, corporate elites whose salaries were in the top two hundred in the country, landscapers and housekeepers who worked for minimum wage, IRS lawyers, schoolteachers, and almost every other type of profession you can imagine. While being predominantly western European Caucasian, the parishes have had significant numbers with Lebanese, Eastern European, Hispanic, African American, Pacific Asian, and Asian backgrounds. Unlike most professional callings, all who are blessed to serve in parish ministry have been blessed (or will be increasingly blessed) to be in community with the broadest cross section of humanity. From new church starts to churches with founding dates of 1693, 1696, and 1705, their histories have been different. I am not alone in the broad diversity of church settings in which I have ministered. All leaders have unique stories about the history and culture of churches they have served.

Because each parish is unique, it’s vital for the new pastor to study the geography, history, and spiritual topography of the particular church’s setting. Questions, questions, and more questions are the essential modus operandi in the start-up phase of a new ministry. Like a child’s how, what, and why questions, the answers to these inquiries will play a important role in shaping the future of the ministry. They help to hasten the process of becoming part of the church family. They help establish future plans and dreams for the church. They highlight sacred cows that, unless detected early, may become stumbling blocks for the growth of new ministry programs.

The church leader needs to remember to study the geography. The lesson plan for this study should include:

- Surveying the property
- Taking a walk around the property
- Talking with those who care for the living and the dead

Early in the ministry, a geography lesson taught by the property manager or custodian or, if appropriate, the chair of the buildings and grounds committee can be beneficial. Knowing the building area is essential as space for programming is being considered. Knowing the major mechanical areas—electrical panels, furnace areas, etc.—can come in handy when a building crisis emerges and both the custodian and head of the property committee are unavailable. Lack of this knowledge can become a time waster. Understanding the building and property plan also allows the pastor or leader to be objective and informed in the midst of budget discussions about property concerns. This knowledge is particularly essential for those churches that lack full-time property management and maintenance staff.

Studying the acreage can also lead to expanded knowledge for outdoor education use and the evangelism ministry. Looking at the property as others see it "from the road" is helpful in creating an inviting campus appearance. Every square inch of property should be seen as potential space for yet-to-be-imagined ministry plans. Space for outdoor meditative chapels and labyrinths, the need for subtle but helpful identification and directional signage, attractive landscaping development, ideas for summer outdoor ministry programs—these are but a few of the ideas that can be generated from surveying the property. The good earth: it is a gift from God to be stewarded and used for the proclamation of the Gospel.

Taking a lengthy walk is a recommended activity for good personal health. Taking a walk is also beneficial for the health of a church. A good healthy walk with the potential for meeting some of the neighbors can nurture an appreciation for the church's ministry. A good walk also provides basic information about opportunities for neighborhood ministry and potential church growth. If the pastor is living in a parsonage on church property, a walk can provide a supportive network of friends from outside of the church.

Getting to know the contiguous neighbors can bring very important insights into the feelings of those neighbors toward the church. These feelings are not always what one might expect. In my "Hello, I'm your neighbor" visits I learned of property-line disputes, concern over the noise that preschool children brought during the day, concerns about traffic in and out of the parking lots, and other less-than-idyllic thoughts about the church's being a neighbor. One church I served was sued because the "noise" from the church bell was "unpleasant and disruptive"! An appropriate but less-than-pastoral response might have been: "The church has been here since the late seventeenth century. That's long before you were here!" But the wisdom from James 1:26 helped me bridle my tongue. Still, most of the boundary-line neighbors were very appreciative of the attempts at being a good neighbor and were supportive of the church's ministry. Being on a first name basis with neighbors can pay large dividends.

A wider-radius investigation is also important for building friendships, expanding ministry offerings, and gathering useful social resources for ministry. Important demographics can be learned by investigating the wider neighborhoods of the community. Senior citizen housing in a neighborhood instead of public schools is a crucial piece of information. Libraries and professional offices might become creative resources for research and outreach ministries. Neighborhood parks and restaurants could provide expanded counseling space for those uneasy with a formal office setting. Taking a mile walk is good for physical health as well as being a body building activity for the Body of Christ.

The Maple Tree

The Maple Tree was a local bar and a luncheon and evening meeting place. It provided the traditional food—burgers, nachos, assorted sandwiches—and for those who imbibed, an assortment of brews. It was also the place where town government officials, members of the trades, a few corporate execu-

> tives, and, during the evening hours, lovers of the blues met to share the music and their life stories. The senior minister of the church I was serving had never dared to enter this den of iniquity. Yet moving blues and good burgers were hard to find so why not pay a visit to the Maple Tree Bar and Grill? Besides, it was a local study in sociology. It was a place where people were freely sharing their life stories; where decisions were being made for the good of the local community; where professional ethics were being debated; where friendships were being built; where music was lifting the spirit. It sounded a lot like church to me. Looking back, I realize that my initial visits to this town landmark provided me with more awareness about the heart of the community than reading the local news and attending town meetings. This also established connections with people who were at the center of what made the town a community. My presence at the Maple Tree opened doors for the church and identified it as a contributor to community vitality. Every community has its gathering places. They can be a rich resource for learning the geography of that community.

For effective ministry there are critical initial visits needed with those who care for the living and the dead:

- *Governmental leaders:* Their plans and decisions affect parishioners and the church.
- *School officials:* They give insights into the family dynamics and youth culture of the community.
- *Hospital administrators, physicians, and nursing leadership:* They are partners in a church's healing ministry.
- *Social service agencies and volunteer support groups*: They provide a glimpse into the needs of the community and offer resources for referral.
- *Funeral directors:* They are partners in one of the most important ministries the church offers. We are centers for death-and-dying ministries.

- *Other clergy:* Attending just one clergy meeting will tell a lot about the state of church life, collegiality, and the influence of the churches in the community.

Knowing the physical and spiritual geography of the church and community is foundational for building a strong Body of Christ.

Sacred Traditions

"Why didn't we sing 'O Lord of Hosts'? You know, in 1905 our organist composed that hymn. Until this year it's been sung on every anniversary Sunday." I thought, on an anniversary Sunday, the power of "God of Grace and God of Glory" would have been just right as the final hymn to send worshippers on their way into the glorious future. I was wrong. Many churches hold certain historical traditions as sacred as the Word of God itself and give identity to themselves through recurring themes in their histories. Oranges for the children on Christmas Eve, historic ties to the first libraries and schools, reading the Salem Covenant of 1630 at every new members' reception, laying claim to the first missionaries to China, Easter sunrise services that always include the same reading written by a beloved deceased minister, the storing of Revolutionary War gunpowder in the church basement, bequests for helping stray dogs—church histories contain everything from the truly historical to the totally hysterical. Local churches have some traditions that if neglected would tear apart one of the threads that binds it together. Usually even the worst traditions are harmless. Some, though, are a source of identity for doing God's work in the world. There is one church where I have worshipped that has a history of dissent against religious and secular authorities. They identify themselves as the *dissenting* church. In the name of righteous dissent they take on much of society's unfair and unjust behaviors. Their primary ministry is to advocate for the poor and marginalized. They are ardent and nearly strident in their fight for justice. They are proud of their motto: "We worship in a spirit of diversity and liberality."

If body building in a church is to be successful, the pastor or leader needs an immersion in basic church history. The curriculum should include:

- Reading historical nonfiction
- Reading a plaque or taking a walk in the local cemetery
- Listening to hoary-headed people
- Seeking the wisdom of colleagues
- Talking with those who went before you

It is true that those who forget the past or neglect the study of history will repeat some of the mistakes of the past. This is a truth to be remembered particularly in church life. History can also lead to a humbling revelation. It allows us to put ourselves in perspective. I have been a pastor of three churches that have celebrated three-hundredth anniversaries. Their longevity and vitality humble me. I am but one of many who have sought to bring the Good News to seekers in my generation. The sooner the family story can be learned, the sooner the pastor can become incorporated into the family. To attain this essential history, the pastor may be fortunate enough to have a church history available. Most local churches have written histories to highlight the church's journey and often report on those times when the church faced division and lost its way. Just as Paul was direct in his critique of the churches he established, most church historians are transparent in their reflections of times of brokenness and separation. For those churches which have not had the opportunity to codify their history in book form, a selected reading of anniversary materials and past church newsletters or annual reports will offer many of the needed insights into the essential historic moments that have helped to define an individual church and its self-understanding.

Rollin Stone, Alva Frisbee, Comfort Starr, Clarence Dunham, Merton Rymph are names on plaques that tell of the story of churches I have served. Some of these individuals are still alive, but most are part of "the church triumphant"—a glorious way of saying "the dead." And whose are these marble chiseled and wood-inlaid names? They include some of the close to one hundred pastors who preceded me in the churches I served. And then there are the cemetery headstones of lay leaders and patron saints of the church; those are also helpful study guides. Most often the key interpreters of these lifeless names are the church historians. They can bring the dead back to life. They can speak of their holiness and their heresies. These historical narratives, particularly of the most recent of predecessors, offer wisdom for the opportunities and challenges ahead.

Don't forget the hoary heads! "The hoary head is a crown of glory, if it be found in the way of righteousness" (Prov 16:31, KJV). It is a term of reverence, for it means frosty or gray-haired, seniors who along life's journey have attained wisdom. Today some may actually be blond or brunette thanks to the hair color industry. But, in spite of the color, we all know a hoary head when we see one. A listening tour to identify longtime members of forty or more years who seem both alert and church savvy can be an insightful experience. Along with gaining trust, we receive valuable knowledge. The efforts pay dividends in times of needed change. These veteran members give honest feedback and wise support. I vividly remember a hundred-year-member offering a very blunt observation: "The only two things that will get you fired are if you're not nice to children and old nuts like me or if you cheat on your wife! We've heard lots of lousy sermons, so you won't lose your job if you can't preach all that well!" She then went on to tell me about ministers who were pushed out because they weren't child friendly or who actually did run off with a member of the church staff. A time to listen to hoary heads will not be ill spent.

While some judicatory officials are leery of advising newly called pastors to contact their predecessors, in most cases it's actually an invaluable tool to get the lay of the land. Some clergy have left a prepared "getting started" resource for the pastor who will follow. The material is written objectively. It does not contain reports about individual church members, which would be too subjective. Information about committee activities, program and administrative information, repetitive church calendar activities, helpful community resources, unfinished program development that will be continuing under lay leadership, and church traditions that have long historic ties can all be very helpful during the transition process.

The most important lessons to be learned focus on the topography of the spirit of individual members. A case in point: the call sermon was completed and the receiving line of well wishers had commenced. Most of the greetings were gracious and nondescript. Warm welcomes and "let me know how I can help" were in abundance. But one church member had more than greetings on his mind. "Welcome . . . hope you'll make the necessary changes here. I especially hope you plan to return the American flag to its place at the front of the sanctuary. Your predecessor removed it during the Vietnam War. Oh, yes, my name is Art Jones. I don't know much about you but I hope we'll become good friends!" All I could think was, okay, point made, but is repositioning the flag a prerequisite for friendship? The next person in line overheard his comments and greeted me warmly by saying: "Don't listen to Art. He's a windbag!" Instantly I could see myself on the horns of a dilemma. But why would Art Jones care about the American flag? I quickly sought out trusted friends from the search committee to educate me about Art Jones. He was a World War II vet, a former town selectman, the son of a former state representative, and his son had attended my alma mater. This was all important information to garner the respect and support of a good-hearted windbag. And yes, I did return the American flag to the front of the sanctuary, for his funeral service only.

Learning the spiritual topography and life stories of each member of the church, at least in a synopsis form, can hasten the partnership between minister and congregation. During the first several months after a new pastor's arrival many churches plan for neighborhood gatherings in members' homes or at the church. It is also helpful to place an insert into the church worship bulletin. The answers to two questions hasten the bonding process.

- What are the four most important things the new pastor should know about you?
- What is one hope or dream you have for our church?

Following their initial home visitation, some log and file notable information about each parishioner. Church family files which include personal notes, news articles, funeral arrangements, etc., are yet another topography-of-the-soul resource. With emerging technologies, secure record keeping is accessible to even the smallest-staffed church. Browsing through the church directory with church leaders can further strengthen the pastor's ties with members.

In a November 2003 *Working Knowledge* newsletter, Harvard Business School professor Michael Watkins, when asked about beginning a new job, answered:

> Leaders, regardless of their level, are most vulnerable in their first few months in a new position. They lack detailed knowledge of the challenges they will face and what it will take to succeed in meeting them. And, they have not yet developed a network of relationships to sustain them. Transitions also are times when small differences in a new leader's actions can have disproportionate impacts on results. Everyone is straining to take the leader's measure and people are forming opinions based on very little information. . . . Failure to create momentum during the first few months guarantees an uphill battle for the rest of their tenure in the job.[1] The long-term success of leaders in any workplace setting is dependent on their start-up strategies. Because of the spiritual and human element in parish ministry, an early immersion in church geography, history, and personal topography is indispensable. Even for the seasoned pastor, just like a GPS, an occasional upgrade is important.

Inspiration

A confused and preoccupied person calls 911 on her cell phone to report that her car had been broken into. She is hysterical as she explains her situation to the dispatcher: "They've stolen the stereo, the steering wheel, the brake pedal, and even the accelerator!" she cries. The dispatcher says, "Stay calm. An officer is on the way." A few minutes later, the officer radioes in: "Disregard. She got in the backseat by mistake." Moral of the story: Be sure you're alert to the geography!

Prayer

God of everywhere, with your help I am here in a particular somewhere. May I come to feel at home in this part of your universe so that I will speak and live out your gracious word in this particular place with its glorious uniqueness. I know that you are with me wherever I may be. Amen.

6

Pastoral Care Is Spelled with Six Ts

"Yes, I Really Do Care!"

Body Building Exercises

- Knowing who you are, what are some of the concerns about your caregiving ministry?
- What are some of the gifts you bring to that ministry?
- How do you see the laity's role in the caregiving ministry?

I felt a close kindred spirit with Greg because he had such an outlandish sense of humor. He had arrived early one evening for a church meeting and came to my office. There was a mischievous grin across his face that made me think I was in for a good laugh: "Bob, I know how much you believe in caring for people. I'm sure there are times when you're counseling someone and you grow tired of listening to them repeat the same old story about how bad their life is. Well I have the perfect thing for you to use at such times." He then dropped a plastic bag on my desk. As I opened it I noticed something that resembled a desk name plate. There was no name on it. Rather, it read "I suppose you think I really care." For a moment I thought it was humorous, but then I found myself almost lecturing Greg: "Even when a person seems to be going nowhere, I really do care! That might be the time I need to care most because it's then that others have grown tired of listening." If there is any ministry the church should hold as paramount, it is the ministry of caregiving. If we think clearly about it, all the ministries of the church are ministries of giving care. There are the comforting words of scripture and the embracing words in a sermon that give insight into finding a peace beyond our understanding. There is the teacher's embrace of a frightened little one in the church school and the attentive ear of a youth group advisor for the heartbroken teenager at being dumped by the love of his life. The church is constantly called to care. The ministry of caring is an all-pervasive ministry. Regardless of the setting, a moment for focused pastoral care might be needed.

In our fast-paced, high-tech, low-touch world, all of us have a deep longing to know that we are cared for, that we are a beloved child of God. I have been an avid viewer of *Saturday Night Live*. One of the characters I found most beguiling was Stuart Smalley, a rather gentle-hearted motivational speaker. At the end of his short segment, Smalley would turn to a mirror and say, “I’m good enough, I’m smart enough, and doggone it, people like me!” Jesus was that mirror for those who felt outcast and broken. As pastors and leaders our role is to be the mirror for all who stand in our presence. We should reflect the truth that each person is a child of God and that he or she is worthy and precious enough to warrant our attention. Jesus’ model of giving care and Paul’s admonition in Romans 12:15 to “Rejoice with those who rejoice, weep with those who weep” are the catalysts for our caring. We are challenged to project to those who feel outcast and broken a presence that says “I am open and ready to listen to and be with you in all seasons of life’s journey.”

We need to spell pastoral care with six Ts as a way of constructing a full-service, compassion-filled ministry of care. The six Ts to be remembered are theology, trust, time, times, teamwork, and tools.

1. Theology

In pastoral-care ministries, our theology must be sound or it will be challenged. We will sometimes be frustrated and depressed because we think we can never do enough. Some couples with marital difficulties with whom we counsel will get divorced. The suffering we see and become immersed in will be overwhelming. Good people will suffer more than they deserve and our words and presence will seem to do little in alleviating their pain. The line between laughter and tears will be thin, and we will be involved in a roller-coaster ride that will pierce our souls and at times might even turn us cynical about God’s love.

In the early years of ministry there is an overwhelming desire to cure people of all their emotional or spiritual diseases. In our training there have been many hours invested in clinical pastoral education and courses in marital counseling, hospital chaplaincy, and death and dying. We feel intellectually ready to heal the sick and raise the dead. Bring it on! Then reality hits: many people who seek counseling are not cured. We play a minor role at best in any physical healings and often experience less-than-miraculous healings of the soul. This reality can be humbling and cause us to question our calling unless we remember we are to bring care, not necessarily cure.

Mora

> Mora was a fourteen-year-old active teen church member who was diagnosed with an aggressive form of leukemia. It was on one of my many visits to her that I learned a very important life lesson. She was lamenting how few of her friends came to visit. As a way of getting the message out through me to her friends she said: "Tell my friends that I may look different and sick, and I am weak, but I know the doctors and nurses will help me get better. My friends think I might die, and that's why they're afraid. I'm sure they don't know what to say. Please tell them they don't have to cure me, just come and be my friend. When they come we can share stories and laugh together." In the Hebrew scriptures one of the terms for healing is *rapha,* which means to bring wholeness and well-being. In the Christian scriptures the Greek word *sozo* is used, and its meaning is to save, to restore the soul and relationships. While in most cases physical health is the ultimate goal, the well-being of the spirit is our primary goal. It is a well-documented fact that being spiritually healthy can be seminal in bringing physical health. We are called to bring spiritual and emotional well-being to those who are touched by our compassionate pastoral care.

Mark's narrative of the paralyzed man being carried to Jesus by his friends helps to clarify the role of caregiver. Jesus tells the paralyzed man to get up and walk because his friends' faith has led to his healing.

Our role in the pastoral care ministry is to help people be moved into the right place for healing. In cases of serious physical disease, the healing might only come because the person finds a spiritual solace and inner strength to fight the illness. It is our role to lift some of the burden, to lighten their load. It is our role to help people see God's light amid the darkness of their pain. We are called to help carry them to a place of spiritual healing and possibly physical healing.

The most challenging theological conundrum we face when called to care is to bring light into the darkness of pain and suffering. The truth is that while we will find ourselves in pastoral moments of great joy, much of our caregiving will be in times of suffering. It is a sobering privilege to be asked into those moments, but it can also be a faith-challenging situation. A significant portion of our ministry will call us to confront the eternal question of "Why suffering?"

William

> It was one of the most difficult and uncomfortable moments in my ministry. I received a call from a friend of the church telling me that her nephew had committed suicide and the family needed me to be with them as they waited for the funeral home to come and remove the body. The suicide scene was horrific, and, as would be expected, the family was angry and grief stricken. I was not alone as comforter and witness to God's presence in this gruesome scene. A well-intentioned aunt of a different theological persuasion than mine kept repeating "God needed William in heaven! It's God's will. It's in His plan." As you might guess, this brought little comfort and even intensified the family's anger toward God. And there I sat, God's ordained representative. It was an incredibly maddening moment. It was then that I once again realized the essential need to develop a definitive theology on the issue of suffering. It was not a time to rush Easter but to honestly address the reality of Good Friday.

Bad things do happen to good and not-so-good people. Sometimes God does seem to be remote when needed most. Consider how many of the Psalms are filled with lamenting and weeping for help. In shaping a "Don't rush to Easter" theology of suffering, I was influenced by the words of the funeral director, nationally acclaimed writer, and friend Thomas Lynch. In reflecting on the tragic death of a thirteen-year-old girl, he addresses all of the easy and not so easy answers: It's God's will; God doesn't tamper with the laws of nature; There is evil in the world and it sometimes rears its ugly head. Being a Catholic, Lynch remembered his mother and her daily recitation of the rosary. His concluding statement is simple yet profound: "Mysteries—like decades of the rosary—glorious and sorrowful mysteries."[1] Amid suffering all we can offer is an acknowledgement of the pain, and help those who suffer to listen for the still small voice that whispers the hopeful words that Easter is coming . A new day of light and resurrection lies beyond the darkness of suffering. Our caregiving needs to be based on a firm theological foundation that understands the difference between care and cure and accepts the mysterious nature and painful reality of Good Friday.

2. Trust

When we spell caregiving, the second T is for trust. Trust is built on two important personal characteristics: attentiveness and confidentiality. I learned a tough lesson early on in my first parish. Because we were blessed with increased worship attendance, the Sunday morning line to greet worshippers became quite lengthy. Realizing that I needed to keep the line moving along, I would unknowingly take a glance out of one eye to see who was coming next so I could be prepared with an appropriate word of welcome. One rather forthright member of the church, who never minced words, said in a loud tone that could be heard by others, "You're not looking at me. I want to trust that you care about me. That might just require ten seconds of eye contact when you're greeting me." Message embarrassingly received! Thus began the ten-second greeting rule. It did not measurably increase the handshaking time but it did nurture the trust that is required if people are to come to you and open every whole and broken part of their lives to you. Pastoral moments can take place at any time and in any place. We must pay attention and let the person in our presence know he or she is a child of God and deserves our full attention.

Sometimes the contact is heart-to-heart over the phone. A friend had called me to talk about her termination from her first full-time pastorate. She was heartbroken. The reason was obvious and had been pointed out to her during a part-time pastorate in another church. It seemed that she loved to gossip, often in the name of expanding the circle of support for struggling members of the church. In her first parish, those visited assumed that confidences shared would be confidences kept. That was not the case. Mistrust began to weaken her pastoral effectiveness and would ultimately lead to a failed ministry.

The reality is that the keeping of confidences is difficult. There is a pastoral urge to share information so that the wider church can become a healing partner. Having the spiritual power of others praying and visiting those with burdens that need to be shared is an important asset in bringing God's comfort to those who are lost and lonely. But in our ministry, when we believe the spiritual power of the whole church would enhance our caring ministry, we must always ask permission before sharing confidences. We are obligated to show our trustworthiness by keeping private issues private. It astounded many of my wife's closest friends when they found out she knew little or nothing about pastoral-care issues going on in the life of the church. Her recurring response to the question "Did you know about . . . ?" was "Bob doesn't tell me; you know it's confidential."

We need to be extremely alert to another reason for breaking confidences, and it is subtle in nature. If our ego becomes weakened, we might share confidential information as a way of building up our own self-importance or as a way of seeking sympathy for the load we must bear. We need to beware of the residue, the harmful effects of our need to be needed. It can lead to an erosion of the trust people put in us.

3. Time

The third T is time. Excellence in pastoral care requires time. Pastoral care is an all-inclusive ministry. As mentioned earlier, organizational structure is an imperative asset in ministry. This is particularly true when it comes to pastoral care. The calls for care and compassion can bombard us. Creatively organizing one's schedule is essential. Regardless of how many others can assist effectively in this ministry, probably a majority of parishioners want their pastor as primary caregiver. Again, creativity in time management is essential. Two of the best time savers are these:

- Schedule in-touch time.
- Use groups for in-touch time.

A valuable practice best in the late afternoon of each workday is to spend an hour either calling or e-mailing members of the church who are lonely or struggling with a personal or family issue. It's the "How are things going?" contact. Occasionally it's just making a general call with no particular issue in mind. In these contacts, a high priority should be placed on the sick and homebound. While some clergy would consider this unnecessary, when on vacation or study leave, I schedule one brief block of time to write one or two lines and send preaddressed and prestamped "thinking of you" postcards. This also expands the ministry of care, and this is particularly appreciated by those who are convalescing or homebound. It enlarges their limited world and serves as a reminder that their church cares. Small blocks of scheduled time for performing seemingly simple acts of care can pay large dividends.

In some churches homebound and convalescent-home lists can be quite lengthy. From personal experience of having up to seventy-five of these saintly souls in parishes I have served, I can assure you that the energy required to keep pastoral care personal is tremendous. After my first several rounds of bimonthly visits to this constituency, I realized that I'd set a visitation expectation that was unsustainable. Because the majority on the list were ambulatory or homebound due to lack of transportation, I decided group visitations could be a time saver. So quarterly group gatherings were scheduled. Part of the group time was focused on updating those attending about what was happening around the church. Occasionally the use of AV resources would augment the personal interaction. The rest of the time was focused on their joys and concerns. Food was often provided by a member of the diaconate who acted as host for the gathering. The group time concept evolved into another group caregiving ministry, "Take a Ride with the Rev." Using either a car or the church van, five to ten homebound members would be picked up for a group outing—to view the fall foliage, catch a museum exhibit, attend a choral event, talk with school children about firsthand accounts of history, spend an hour at the senior center visiting with friends. One of these ventures in pastoral care must have been record setting. On a visit to a local park with a group that included one eighty-five-year-old, three eighty-eight-year-olds, one ninety-six-year-old and one ninety-seven-year-old, all rode on the carousel. Doctor permission slips were not required! Through using the group concept, clergy visitation hours were saved as those in the car or on the van talked, listened, visited, and ministered to each other.

Group visitations that required not more than a couple of hours rather than one-on-ones that could take many more hours; being the voice on the end of the line at the end of the day; being a catalyst for building support groups for singles, the bereaved, or people in similar health and life situations—these and other creative options for giving care can revitalize our ministries and save time on our overloaded schedules.

4. Times

In a world on overdrive where the present and future seem to simultaneously occupy our attention, there needs to be a place that remembers the times of passage in our lives. There needs to be a place that stops us in our tracks and allows us to breathe in the aromas of the past, and reminds us from where we came and whose we are. Many of the higher liturgical churches have learned how to ritualize significant moments from the past. Many of the less liturgical churches have lost some of the pastoral power of remembering through liturgy. Creating times to remember is an important pastoral ministry. Naturally, remembering and acknowledging a significant life passage through personal contact is best. This, of course, requires a commitment to keep track of those life passages. Technology is an important tool in organizing the personal pastoral-care ministry. A phone call to a couple who were married the previous year can lead to a renewed relationship with the church and a "thank you" for remembering—and thank you to Microsoft Organizer for digitally bringing to mind their nuptials. Social media can help us mark passages; everybody seems to have their birthday on Facebook! I experienced a Facebook ministry opportunity the other evening. I was logged into my own Facebook account when what should appear but a wedding photo with a young clergyman officiating who looked suspiciously like I did thirty years ago. A congratulatory comment was sent to the couple in the space of fifteen seconds.

Along with the standard sharing of information through church media, we need to look at ways to revitalize the historic forms of ritualizing life passages and new creative liturgical forms of marking these moments. On Remembrance Sunday (All Saints' Day), have spouses and relatives of the deceased saints to be remembered select their loved ones' favorite hymns. This will serve to bring alive the "cloud of witnesses" that surround us. On the Sunday of the Festival of the Christian Home (Mother's Day), encourage families to bring photos of themselves at favorite vacation spots. Display them on easels throughout the sanctuary or include them in the bulletin. Project on a screen or whiteboard their favorite words of advice or saying about the blessings of being family. Create brief liturgical moments that ritualize the emotions that are present at times of graduation, job loss or gain, aging, or relocation. The possibilities for revitalizing tired rituals of passage are manifold.

Remembering

> The woman came to me asking if I would lead a chapel service of remembrance for those parents who had experienced the death of infants or toddlers. The suggested date was near Mother's Day. "We want to remember our angels. So many people think we want to forget and as time goes by it becomes easier to forget, but we need the healing of remembering

> and hearing their names spoken." The service was both heart wrenching and therapeutic for the participants. Music, scripture, a time to offer stories, and candles lighted for each child were each a part of the service. These parents gave a face and spiritual depth to what suffering and resurrection mean. One woman lighted eight candles representing her number of miscarriages and stillborn births. Yet she rejoiced in the miracle of one successful birth, her twin daughters. She proclaimed a message of hope that few of our best sermonic efforts could match.

Simply and elaborately designed labyrinths are being built on the property of an increasing number of churches. Written resources to be used by couples, widows and widowers, and those in life transitions as they walk on their quiet journey can be effective tools for caregiving. Couples walking individually into the center of a labyrinth can be encouraged to reflect on their past together: how they met, what were the joys they experienced and the struggles they had overcome. As they walk out together they can reflect on what God is calling them to do as a couple to strengthen their marriage and to witness to others about the sacredness of their covenant. Spiritual resources for those significant rites of passage can be designed in written and technology-based forms. They can highlight life passage moments and bring spiritual insight and God's grace to the remembrance of those moments. Imagine a hand-held device full of downloaded resources with guided meditations and music that focus on loss and renewal for the bereaved. These could also focus on faith-based parenting skills for a new parent and could be played on a morning walk or jog. In a world that has lost its ability to stop and remember life passages, the church needs to be the place where we remember those holy moments.

5. Teamwork

The call came at 2:00 a.m. The voice on the other end of the line sounded as if the caller had already drunk way too much alcohol; to put it even more bluntly, he sounded stone cold drunk. The thirty-two-year-old man had a history of battling alcoholism. "I think I'm going to kill myself. My parents are away on vacation and I'm really, really confused. Just thought I'd call to talk with you." Instead of a lengthy conversation which would have led us down the same path we had followed before, I told him I was on my way. Before changing into street clothes I made two phone calls. The first was to Frank, a church member and also a member of the 7:00 a.m. AA group that met at the church. My only words to Frank were: "You know the deal! See you at 133 Winthrop Road in fifteen minutes." The next call was to the police station. "Hi, this is Bob Naylor. Who's this?" "Bob, it's Dave." My rather terse response was: "Dave, hope all things are good with you. Is Liza on neighborhood patrol tonight?" "Nope, it's Frank tonight!" was Dave's matter-of-fact response. Great, I thought to myself, a totally blasted drunk having to figure out which Frank is which. I told Dave the story and asked him to have Frank, the police officer, meet me at the same house in fifteen minutes. "I think it's best if he waits outside until I get there. The person we need to help should first see a familiar face." Fifteen minutes later we met and planned our strategy. It was a successful intervention, and the young man was taken by Frank and me to the ER for admittance into the drug and alcohol rehab unit.

The point of the story is not about the success of the intervention but rather about having a team in place. Within fifteen minutes, a crisis was being addressed effectively. An AA member and church member who arrived at church every morning at 7:00 a.m. to be supported in his sobriety; seventeen police officers' whose names, personalities, and expertise were learned through visits to the police station—little did they know they would become part of the pastoral-care team. The word "teamwork" is the fifth T in pastoral care.

We who are called to take the lead in the ministry of pastoral care cannot do it alone. It is too overwhelming and draining. We should not try to do it alone if we are to lead a church that is comprehensive in its ministry of care. As mentioned previously, it is important to establish ties with community resources such as healthcare professionals and community support agencies. It's a good practice to identify and, through prayerful vetting, build a team of people with expertise in areas that bring essential skills to the caregiving ministry. Nurses, doctors, lawyers, therapists, social workers, professional educators, addiction consultants, research librarians, financial experts, and even artists can all become part of the healing team. With this team approach, the pastor becomes the spiritual guide, as well as the resource coordinator. Many of these experts will self-identify by their participation as church members. Others become part of the team through a formal request, such as a simple "Will you help if a situation arises that needs a person with your expertise?" Asking is often all that is needed to secure the help of a potential team member. Occasionally a barter system can be worked out to add members to the team: building trust with a doctor and offering our visitation and extensive spiritual care skills in exchange for health-related expertise in helping families struggling with illness; being a resource on ethics for a financial firm in exchange for an occasional budgeting consultation with a family under extreme financial pressures; offering artists display space and even studio space at the church in exchange for involvement in the arts for individuals dealing with extreme stress. Building a team of caregivers by enlisting a wide range of relationships can broaden the caregiving network. The team concept will be strengthened when its members know they are considered an important part of the team while utmost confidentiality is required. The basic foundation of any effective program of pastoral care is the laity. Their roles include:

- Conduits of information
- On-the-ground communicators of care
- Specialized caregivers and visitors

In our age of extensive communication, people often assume that the pastor is fully informed of everyone's need. That is not always the case. An example is ministry in a hospital setting. With rigid privacy regulations and an increasing number of day surgeries and short-term hospital stays, it is easy for a parishioner's care to be overlooked. All lay persons must see themselves as conduits of information about other members. Church media resources should encourage sharing with the pastor of basic information about members in healthcare and rehabilitation facilities and other significant personal and family situations Creating multiple avenues for encouraging and receiving pastoral concerns is essential because there is often a pervading assumption that "Of course, the pastor knows about. . . ." It is supportive of the ministry when members see themselves as conduits of situations where pastoral ministry could be helpful.

It is also valuable to remind the whole church membership that they are the front line of pastoral care. Several times a year it's a good practice to insert in the church newsletter or Sunday bulletin articles that encourage the whole membership to participate in pastoral care. Articles that provide basic information about the skills needed for effective caregiving, such as listening skills or intercessory prayers for use in a home setting, will strengthen the members' abilities to be more effective in all of their interpersonal relationships. Church-developed online courses in the art of caregiving can empower the laity to be more effective in their general caregiving. The use of the homebound for intercessory prayer and phone visitation expands the ministry of care, while giving a deeper sense of purpose to those unable to participate fully in the church's witness. The homebound can also become effective agents to welcome new members into the church and to share their life stories and the folklore of the church. It only requires a telephone contact.

A key component of comprehensive pastoral care is an expansion of the base of trained laity who are able and willing to supplement the pastor's efforts. The words of a committed but emotionally overloaded pastor give evidence to this need: "Bob, in all honesty, I sometimes want to sequester myself away and forget about having to care. There's not a person in life who doesn't have a hurt that needs healing or a fear that needs to be calmed. I'll be honest with you, sometimes I stare into people's eyes as if I am listening, but I am not hearing a thing. I want to care, but I can't." Because all of our involvements in people's lives will require a healing word of hope, grace, or support it is invaluable to have a team of trained laity to support us in our ministry of care.

A surprising number of church members already have the gifts to be set apart for this ministry. There are a few key ingredients needed to equip these volunteers. While many lay training courses are available outside of the local church, a simple class can easily be designed for either individual or interchurch training. Often dominations have their own resources. My denomination, the United Church of Christ, has an excellent resource, *Called to Care.* With any local churched designed or predesigned training program there are basic elements that need to be included.

- Establish ground rules of respect for confidentiality, sharing information with the pastor, and knowing when to step back.
- Learn how to get out of the way and really listen by setting aside personal agendas and stories, and learning how to listen in earnest.
- Determine ways to acquire basic knowledge about healthcare so there's a fundamental understanding of the illness and the caregiving dos and don'ts in each health-related environment.
- Become familiar and comfortable with faith resources; it's essential to feel at ease with the use of scripture and prayer.
- Recognize and commission the trained caregivers; the congregation needs to know those who are set apart for this ministry so they may affirm their efforts.

As pastors and leaders of churches, we will need help if we are not to be overwhelmed by the cries for help and healing. Teamwork equals success.

6. Tools

The sixth T is tools. As Christians we have an expanded toolbox for our ministry of care. For several years it was my privilege to be the judicatory endorser and supporter of those serving in nonparish settings: pastoral counselors, hospital chaplains, and counselors in military and federal correctional institutions. It was always my worry that these specialized ministers in secular settings might fail to use Christian resources in their ministries. One pastoral counselor confessed: "I go light on talking about faith and using resources that have a faith emphasis. Sometimes religion has been part of the client's problem." While such an attitude may reflect the thinking of a small minority of those who serve in specialized settings, we need to remember that people who come to us believe we do have spiritual resources that can heal their broken souls. People come to us looking not only for mental health but also spiritual health. Our spiritual toolboxes are filled with many resources:

- *Scripture:* devotionals based on scripture and reflective resources
- *Prayer:* a plethora of prayer forms from a broad range of historic faith traditions
- *Healing touch:* a sensitive area, since touch has been used to abuse; however, used with discretion, it is a valuable part of the church's ministry
- *Arts:* visual, musical, dramatic, written: all important tools as doorways to the soul
- *Humor:* the gift that allows us to stand at a safe distance and view ourselves as we laugh at human foibles
- *Wider mission:* a focus on the concerns and needs of others rather than ourselves
- *Meditative space:* sanctuary, quiet space with the healing gift of silence for meditation, often providing a sense of greater intimacy for the journey to spiritual health and physical healing
- *A physical or cyberspace forum:* for example, CaringBridge, to share information about specific physical, emotional, or relational illnesses—frequently needed as a means of empowerment as persons try to take control of their illness

All of us have snapshots of what pastoral care looks like. The remembrance of these moments inspires us and emboldens us to care again and again. Here are some representative snapshots:

- Pat and Arnold were having a heated moment in their marriage counseling session. Voices were being raised and blaming fingers were pointed at each other. The pastor spoke with firmness: "Enough shouting. It's time for a little prayerful silence." During that silence the words of Paul's definition of love were quietly spoken: "Love is patient and kind. . . ." The voice paused and said,

"After each verse, I'm going to let each of you confess—that's right, confess—when you didn't act out Christian love." What followed was painful but revelatory and redemptive.

- Janet had come seeking solace and was obviously depressed. The minister gave her the nonjudgmental listening she needed. As she was ready to leave he gave her a comedy DVD with a devotional resource which he had created to complement the movie. It included scripture and prayers.
- Allison was a teenager battling a drug abuse problem. While seeing a therapist she still seemed to gravitate to her pastor's office, as she said, to check in. As they talked, she revealed her love of pen-and-ink cartoon drawing. After further conversation, her pastor confidently asked if she would design the cover for the Sunday bulletin. The day's scripture would guide her work. After she completed her drawing, they discussed her biblical interpretations.
- A woman came forward at the conclusion of the healing service and requested a special laying on of hands on her head. After countless doctors' visits and a myriad of tests, she had been diagnosed with a nonmalignant brain tumor. It would require risky surgery. After the laying on of hands, she seemed more at ease as she exited the chapel.
- Youth group members, their advisors, and parents gathered at 7:00 p.m. to pray for Megan. Their youth group friend was hospitalized with a rapidly progressing, uncontrollable, and undefinable bacterial infection. Even the doctors and nurses felt a miracle was the only hope. At precisely 7:00 p.m. her vital signs began to improve. Her healthcare professionals were amazed at the steady and rapid turnaround. The prayer vigil continued through the night. By the next day she was moved from ICU to a limited care room on the medical floor of the hospital.
- Beth and Jim had been struggling with their relationship. After joining others of the church family serving dinner at the homeless shelter, they began to realize how blessed they were. Their

marital struggles seemed to lessen. One could only hope that this other- focused ministry helped to renew their marriage.

As pastors and leaders we are blessed with a vast toolbox of resources for our ministry of care and healing. We are called by God to effectively and creatively use all of them. We are called to care so voraciously and compassionately that those who receive our ministry know that God is absolutely in their midst.

Our lives should be a testimony that we really care and that all who are overburdened or have heavy hearts can come to us to be connected to Jesus who offers us rest. (See Appendix A, Weekly Pastoral Care Contact Checklist.)

Inspiration

Protestant minister and writer Frederick Buechner sums it up: "Compassion is the sometimes fatal capacity for feeling what it is like in somebody else's skin. It is a knowledge that there can never be any peace and joy for me until there is peace and joy for you too."[2]

Prayer

Healer of the sick and lame, Comforter of the broken hearted and lost, Releaser of those who are locked up in fear, help me to care when I don't have any more energy. Help me to listen when the stories become repetitious or disjointed. Grant me the courage to get close when others keep their distance. Give me faith so that through my caring others will feel touched by the healing Spirit of Jesus. Amen.

7

Invited In Where Others Cannot Go

Hatching, Matching, and Dispatching – Sacred Moments in Pastoral Care

Body Building Exercises

It's Thursday and you're in the midst of struggling with the text for Sunday's sermon—it just doesn't seem to be going anywhere. Your 11:00 a.m. Bible study is on schedule, and that will surely be lively and probably run past the allotted hour. This evening you have a stewardship campaign meeting and you've been asked to draft a sample cover letter for the chair to consider and edit or rewrite. A luncheon meeting with a potential new member is scheduled for 12:30 p.m. You had planned to use most of the early afternoon to make some progress on the sermon and get the stewardship meeting materials organized. The rest of the day was set aside for attending your son's afterschool soccer game. You had promised him you'd be there. But you had promised that before and missed the game. The phone rings and on the other end of the line there's a sobbing voice. It's the voice of an inactive middle-aged member. The past few weeks you had been visiting her husband at the hospital. "He's dead! He died about an hour ago. I can't believe it. The doctor had told me he was improving. I just wanted you to know. It's devastating!"

- What do you do?
- What principles guide your decision?
- What do your decisions say about your priorities?
- How will you deal with undone priorities?

The fullest implementation of the six Ts of pastoral care will be most challenged at the times of hatching, matching, and dispatching. Those of us who are called to take the lead in pastoral care are blessed with the privilege of being invited into people's lives at seminal moments. No other profession is given access to the lives of individuals and families at deeply emotional, sacred moments. We are welcomed at times of birth (hatching), marriage (matching), and illness and death (dispatching). We become a part of the extended family and are given access to the hidden places in people's lives. Because of this privilege we should be humble in spirit and comprehensive in our care ministry. We are called to be the experts in things related to hatching, matching, and dispatching. Once when asked what I meant by the comprehensive nature of our care in these areas, I responded: "We should know everything from how to hold a baby's head comfortably in our arms at the time of baptism to where the head of the casket is as we carry it out of the sanctuary at the time of the funeral. We should know the spiritual and emotional investments required for a great variety of issues, from a successful marriage to the financial outlay to pay for a funeral." Individuals and families will call on us to be their guides through the joys and sorrows of these emotionally charged times of life's journey.

Baptism

There is immense joy that comes with hatching! While there will be those moments of the dark night of the soul when we are called to walk through a problem pregnancy or a stillbirth, there usually will be overwhelming joy and thanksgiving at the time of a birth. We are privileged to be participants in that joy. But we are also to bring a spiritual presence into a sacred moment which is often transformed into a largely secularized celebration. Amid the balloons and teddy bears and beaming relatives we are to announce the love of God in the midst of it all. This can become particularly obvious at the time of the baptism, that time when some parents come to church to have the baby "done," to have the rite of passage completed on the checklist of life. Often the baptism is the parents' first return to the church since their own marriage. Many of the secularized faithful have little understanding of the seriousness of the commitment that comes with baptism.

The pastor should be concerned about making the celebration *sacred* and about incorporating the child fully into the family of faith. Along with parents' promises there is also the congregation's promise to give their love, support, and care to the child and the family as the child grows in the faith. As a way to stimulate your creativity, here are possible approaches for making the celebration of a birth a sacred moment:

- *Gifts at the time of a birth:* a baby's Bible included in a gift package taken either to the hospital or the home soon after the birth. With this gift is information about the meaning of the sacrament of baptism, a devotional on the Christian family, information concerning the church's children's (and preschool) ministry program and, in the case with older siblings, a Bible coloring book or an age-appropriate Bible storybook.
- *Announcement of the birth:* an altar rosebud presented during the worship service. The rosebud is delivered to the family by a deacon or church member, thus beginning the incorporation process. When a church member has volunteered to be a spiritual grandparent, that person delivers the rosebud.
- *Welcoming the infant into the church school:* handmade cards from the children. Ask the parents of a toddler to reach out to the new parents. A resource that includes information about childcare options, daycare opportunities, mother or parents' groups sponsored by the church or other community agencies attests to the fact that the church has an extensive support system for young families. One of the most important ministries a church can offer families with infants is a well-lighted, clean and inviting infant-care space. Well-trained childcare volunteers and pagers or text messaging capabilities to contact worshipping parents if they are needed make an overt statement that we are privileged to welcome the child into your family. If there are any rooms that require constant attention and refurbishing it's always the infant, toddler, and preschool areas. Within the first three months after the birth, a resource describing the mean-

ing of baptism, church practices and requirements for this sacrament, and a sample baptismal liturgy should be mailed.

- *Guidelines for maintaining the sanctity of the moment at the time of the sacrament:* preprinted cards for the parents to share with others regarding photographs. Each pastor or church needs to establish the policy. I have allowed existing light photographs from a designated seating area. I have also made myself available for photographs following the worship service. The triangular nature of the sacrament—the covenant among the parents, church family, and God—needs to be made clear. A visual act of bringing the child into the midst of the worshipping congregation should be considered. Ways to help parents remember their promises might also be included at this time. In my parish we have done this in a unique way, which has tied together mission and sacrament. Disadvantaged youth from a local pottery center create and fire clay bowls that are used for the baptism and subsequently given to the family as a reminder of their vows. Another gift we have given is a CD of lullabies performed by our minister of music. Some are based on much-loved hymn tunes.
- *A presence following the baptism*: Along with regular contacts by the church school and adult members, a letter could be sent at the time of the baptismal anniversary. It is a privilege to be invited into the joyously sacred moment of birth. We are challenged to bring blessing to that moment while also beginning the incorporation process into the family of faith so the child may become a faithful follower of the One we call Savior.

Marriage

The voice on the other end of the line seemed frenetic. “Hello, this is Jim James and I’ve been dating this great woman. We’ve decided to get married and would like to do it as soon as possible. My cousin is a member of your church, and she told me to contact you about officiating.” This was going to be my first wedding, but something bothered me about the rush to marriage. The need for an immediate wedding raised some red flags—Pregnant? Fighting over a family's disapproval? Rush before a military deployment? I made no promises except to say that I wanted to talk with the couple before making a decision. Jim agreed, and when he and Betty, his fiancée, arrived for the premarital meeting I suddenly fully understood the urgency. This was not a shot-gun wedding. This was rather a "we've got a short time" wedding. Jim and Betty were well into their senior years—eighty-nine and eighty-three, to be exact.

Two weeks later, a family who had marginal involvement as church members called with a similar request for my officiating at what was to be a lavish wedding. It seemed that the couple was into historical reenactments and wanted a wedding complete with Colonial costumes and worship style. There would be twenty-eight in the bridal party. I acknowledged that I could provide a Colonial liturgy and that I could handle a bridal party of gargantuan proportions. But I also said emphatically, "No! I will not wear a Colonial costume!"

On another occasion, the scene in my office was difficult. The young woman from a very prominent family in the community was having a huge disagreement with the man she was to marry in five weeks' time. His voice was raised in an attack on her family's less-than-affirming attitude about him. Prayerfully and haltingly I said, "I would strongly suggest postponing the marriage and having some couple counseling, or cancelling the wedding altogether!" The silence that followed was deafening. Thousands of dollars had been invested in this high society nuptial. We said little more except to set another meeting two days later. We prayed together and concluded our premarital session. Two days later the wedding was cancelled.

These are but three of the diverse stories that have come from counseling and officiating at over seven hundred and fifty weddings. Add twenty-three other couples who were counseled into not tying the knot. There has been great joy, much laughter, and some raw sadness in overseeing the rite in which a community of faith brings its blessing to a marriage. Early on in my ministry I realized that my essential roles in the matching process were:

- To provide the resources for a faithful and healthy marriage in which promises are kept "until death do us part."

- To navigate the couple through the liturgical process so that the wedding is a sacred celebration of selfless love rather than a soap-opera-style show or merely a passing chapter in a shallow romance novel.

It also became clear that parameters about participation in a wedding need to be established by those who officiate. Guidelines might include:

- The presence of a Christian clergyperson acknowledges the presence of the triune God in the service.
- A couple must have two to four premarital sessions with the pastor or in a group setting. No walk-in or "rush" weddings! In ecumenical or interfaith settings, the sharing of the premarital sessions may be established in concert with the other officiating religious representative.
- After the second session it is the pastor's prerogative to decide whether or not to participate in the ceremony. In questionable situations, helping to lead the couple to a mutual decision for postponement or cancellation is essential.
- In multiple-staff settings, ordained colleagues on staff will officiate at weddings when requested by a member of the church and should be called on to share in nonmember weddings.
- Only the pastor has the right to officiate at church weddings. The pastor may waive that responsibility in situations where it seems appropriate. Familiarity with the liturgy, the custodial and music staff, and the building layout is important in the smooth oversight of a wedding and is best left to the home pastor. Often if the couple lives in a community, the nurturing of the marriage becomes the responsibility of the host pastor. However in obvious situations, co-officiating should be encouraged.
- On occasion special considerations should be given to officiating at weddings outside of the sanctuary.
- In ecumenical or interfaith weddings, participation requires full respect for the traditions of both the bride and the groom.

- The pastor will officiate when there has been a divorce. Candor about the realities of the previous marriage should be revealed to the pastor.
- Like any marriage ceremony, a same-sex wedding should receive the blessing of the church. Pastors not inclined to conduct same-sex weddings should make every effort to assist the couple in finding a pastor who would officiate.
- Even in situations of couples who have been living together, the extent of premarital counseling will remain the same.

It is essential to have established parameters before being called to the matching ministry so that the pastor and church's integrity can be upheld. A periodic reflection on and review of these is extremely important in light of the constantly changing societal patterns and legal requirements that surround marriage today. In is beneficial to discuss these issues with the appropriate lay board that oversees the sacraments and rites of the church.

With the increasing rate of divorce, it is essential that those who place the stamp of approval on the matching of two people then provide them resources for a faithful and healthy marriage. The premarital sessions provide the beginning of this firm foundation-building process. It might be helpful if the initial meeting is seen as a time to demythologize romantic love and replace it with the selfless love—*agape*—of Jesus Christ. As I have often said to couples, "Marriage is not always the easiest way to live, but it is the most fulfilling way to live. It will bring serendipitous joys and challenging trials. But through both, you will experience a love that is beyond all understanding."

Often some of the deepest issues about a relationship have only been partially addressed or have been avoided totally in the lead-up to the marriage—the "We will get to that later" avoidance issue. Rather, the premarital session should be open and forthright in addressing the following:

- *Faith:* Since the couple has come to a Christian setting for the wedding, the mysteries of Christian love need to be discussed.

The concept of "leave taking" from a single (often me-centered life) to an other-centered life requires some serious attention. The lifetime commitment that is required to fully experience *agape*, servant love, should be underscored.

- *Finances and chosen lifestyle:* Unless the realities of the material world are addressed and put into a spiritual context, they are likely to bring tension to a marriage. The gift of simplicity and the hazards of waiting to have it all should be discussed with honesty.
- *Sexuality and children:* The physical relationship needs to be discussed. In a world that has so many misunderstandings about sexuality and what the church believes on the issue, a forthright discussion is essential. The physical relationship is a gift from God and therefore is an extension of the spiritual relationship. Having an honest discussion between the premarital sessions on how each views the physical relationship should be urged. A time of addressing the issue of their desires about having children and the joys and challenges of sustaining a loving couple relationship while being attentive and loving in their parenting can bring healthy insights into the building of a Christian family.
- *Time and communication:* A blessed marriage calls for effective and constant communication. Tools for expressing a love that is patient and kind, that uplifts, needs to be offered. Techniques for blocking out time for one-to-one communication and the use of technology for enhancing communication—i.e., texting affection—might be discussed. Naturally scripture and devotional resources that could be utilized in "couple time" should be made available.

As mentioned earlier, one of the most challenging aspects of a clergyperson's role in the rite of Christian marriage is to be certain the liturgy becomes a sacred celebration of Christian love and commitment and not an entertaining sideshow. In their decision to have a Christian wedding, whether knowingly or not, couples have asked for just that—a *Christian* wedding! Therefore these issues need to be discussed.

- *Deciding about the place of the service:* Unless there is a deep spiritual tie to a specific geographic location or a discomfort in an interfaith wedding with the overwhelming presence of a sanctuary's Christian symbolism, a church ceremony should be the preferred option.
- *Selecting scripture and blending with compatible secular readings:* Any wedding resources compiled should include a listing of appropriate scripture for use in the ceremony. If family or friends are the lay readers for the scripture, ample time at the rehearsal should be taken for practice in reading the text with proper inflection and clarity.
- *Having present the word and sacrament:* A brief personal reflection on scripture should be given serious thought. The inclusion of the sacrament of Communion should be discussed. While some would disagree, receiving Communion by the couple alone (while others spiritually reflect on the meaning of the sacrament) might be appropriate. On the other hand, an open Communion table can make a powerful statement about Christian sacrifice and service. This can be dramatically symbolized by the couple serving the elements to their family and friends. Beware: it is best if the bride serves the bread; wine or a drop of grape juice stains wedding gowns.
- *Including symbolic acts and their translation into a Christian context:* The remembrance of much-beloved family and friends who are unable to attend the ceremony for reasons of health or because they have died is easily wrapped into the context of a "cloud of witnesses." By their examples they have taught the couple the nuances of Christlike love. Unity candles can become the Christ candle.
- *Bringing the attendees on board.* A significant number of those attending the wedding may very well have no understanding of their role and responsibility in the sacred celebration. While a minority may have some sense of the sacredness of the celebration, most feel they are an audience for a romantic soap opera or are there because it would seem inappropriate to show up only for

the reception and open bar. They need to be educated that they, by their presence, affirm the union. Clergy officiate, but the gathered community affirms the marriage. One way to accomplish this is to use a unison marriage pronouncement ("We pronounce you").

- *Keeping it simple:* Early on in the premarital preparation, a word for simplicity needs to be spoken. We are well aware that the marriage industry is a primary force behind the shaping of the wedding day: times set around restaurant or club availabilities; wedding consultants; photographers' photo ops before and after the wedding. We need to be a countervailing force in the planning process. In essence it could be said that a wedding license, supportive witnesses, and an affirmation by the couple to love and to cherish in the spirit of Christ "as long as they both shall live" is all that is required for the solemnization of a marriage. And it can all be performed in the minister's office. A couple, a community of faith gathered, someone to officiate, recognition of God's Spirit, promises of covenantal commitments—that's all it takes. Tuxedos, long flowing gowns, and costly receptions may be nice but too often are excessive. Having family and friends create a simple and sacred time should be the challenge offered by the pastor. For those who sincerely wish to make a statement about their faith, a registry of outreach and mission organizations in lieu of wedding gifts provides a powerful example of what is truly important in the couple's relationship.
- *Handling the production team:* A humorist once said, "You'll want to buy a lot of pictures of your wedding so your family and friends can see what happened while the photographer was in their way." Photographers, videographers, transport services, wedding coordinators, and, yes, even parents are often the production team with which the pastor must deal. Therefore we need to be ready to simultaneously demonstrate that we are in charge while appreciating the roles of others who are assisting in creating the perfect wedding. Either at the premarital counseling or at the rehearsal, consider distributing printed reminders for each of the production team members. Their roles will be clearly defined, and this

announces to them who is in charge. In a humorous but straightforward way, they need to know the minister is in charge of the sacred ceremony and the church space. A map of the best photography views, without being intrusive, goes a long way in dealing with the most prevalent cause of diminishing the sanctity of the celebration, the photographer. Also the way we oversee the rehearsal sets the tone not only for the wedding party but for the parents, coordinators, and, photographers. Doses of organization, warmth, humor, and prayer are the elements that set the tone at the rehearsal.

We have been given the special privilege of bringing two people together in the shared journey of marriage. We oversee the making of sacred covenants. Let us be faithful conduits of the spiritual and practical insights needed to make for a successful and faith-filled matching.

Death and Dying

"Life is pleasant. Death is peaceful. It's the transition that's troublesome." These words of the author Isaac Asimov speak of the sacred territory into which we are invited and in which our skills of pastoral care are most challenged.[1] We are invited into the death-and-dying space. There is no more profound privilege given us than to be welcomed into this awesome, beautiful, frightening, and, might we say, holy time. As one dying man told me, "I ask you to be by my side as I write this final chapter of my life on this side of the grave. Please help me to make this chapter reflect beauty and courage." All I could say in response to these heartfelt words was, "You honor me by your request. Let the writing begin."

Why are we invited in? It is because we have chosen a calling that in the end deals with the most important questions that reside deep within the soul of every human being: "What am I to do with this gift of life?" and "How am I to live knowing that I will die?" In the somewhat whimsical language I have been using, we are called to help dispatch with love and dignity a human spirit into the chapter of life after this earthly life. Our roles in this holy ministry include:

- To be a light-bearer at all times while walking with another in the shadows
- To be a facilitator and mediator in sticky and tough places
- To be an overseer of the rite of passage
- To be a shoulder to lean on while walking lame and learning to speak the language

The revered Rabbi Abraham Joshua Heschel reflected on facing death: "The greatest problem is not how to continue [our existence] but how to exalt our existence. The cry for life beyond the grave is presumptuous, if there is no cry for eternal life prior . . . to the grave. Eternity is not perpetual future but perpetual presence. God has planted within us the seed of eternal life. The world to come is not only a hereafter but a *herenow*."[2] Heschel's remarks coalesce comfortably with the teachings of another rabbi, Jesus of Nazareth. He too spoke of the hereafter through the resurrection from the dead but also of living fully in the here and now—"The dominion of God is in your midst!" Our primary role is to assist those who are physically healthy, as well as those who are in the dying process, to live eternally in the here and now.

To be beacons of light while walking with others through the dark is imbedded in our entire ministry. From the words that we speak from the pulpit to the funeral arrangement checklists and the advanced directive documents that are accessible in the brochure holders throughout the church, our ministry's underlying motto is to live fully, to live in the light knowing you will die. From workshops with funeral directors, healthcare professionals, and lawyers about the death-and-dying process to the promotion of healthy lifestyles, we challenge the members of our congregations to choose life. "I call heaven and earth to witness against you today that I have set before you life and death, blessings and curses. Choose life so that you and your descendants may live" (Dt 30:19). Even when death is imminent, we choose life.

Olga

> Olga was a heroic soul who had faced life-threatening illness on several occasions. As I sat by her bedside when the time of her death was looming, she opened her eyes and said to me, "Continue to tell me the stories of the day and make me laugh. I am on the final journey, but damn it, I'm still alive!" She challenges all of us who enter into the dying process to treat those who still have breath as still being among the living. Often we are concerned with our need to be *the one* with whom the dying share their deepest feelings. We are to be attentive to moments when the need to express regrets and fears appear, and unanswered questions surface. But life—past and present—is our agenda otherwise. We need to talk of what is happening in the world. We need to encourage children and pets (when allowed) to be part of the care team. When appropriate and with the approval of medical professionals, we might move with the person to a brighter and more comfortable place for our time with them. It is light and abundant life that we bring.

I once heard a humorous story about a member of the clergy who was on his deathbed. Family and friends had gathered around. They believed he was in a coma. They began to praise his ministry. One person highlighted his compassion, another his patience, another his oratorical abilities, another his intellect. Once they had finished a rather lengthy litany, the pastor's eyes opened and he said in a still clear voice, "You forgot my humility!"

The dying need to know that their lives have had meaning. By our words encouraging them to recount the meaningful stories of their lives, by asking others to share their memories, by having them journal or record their life story, we can be the catalyst to see that their life mattered. In some situations even encouraging the family to write the person's obituary with them can be therapeutic. Reflecting on the fruit of the Spirit with the dying and having them remember those moments when theirs bore fruit is but one way to draw on scripture in this ministry of meaning.

As bearers of light we must always bear witness to hope in the promises. By our deportment we witness to hope. With occasional moments of laughter, we help the person to laugh at life and not fear death. With the recitation of the Psalms or the mantra-like repetition of verses of scripture we can bring calm and hope to a struggling soul. Sometimes we will need to be a counterbalance to the negativity that does not bring comfort. We attempt to facilitate the hope of reconciliation in families where there is separation. Through the bringing of church-school children's artwork into the person's sight, we can offer the hope and simple joy that innocent love can carry. Our ministry is built on the foundation of hope in new life.

We are also called to walk through Good Friday with those who are dying. We are called to be comfortable with darkness. We are called to model for loved ones how to be at peace and act in darkness. Many fear darkness and keep their distance from pain. We get close so the dying know that they are not alone. We touch, in ways coordinated with healthcare professionals, so that they realize that in spite of their broken body, we still see the beauty in their being. We listen attentively so the dying know that what they have to say is important. With attentiveness we can then shape our prayers to address the soul issues they are facing. We who are trained to speak are challenged to now listen patiently, no matter how painful or how long the silence. Accepting and proclaiming the reality of Good Friday is in our pastoral-care portfolio.

Usually those who are sick or dying have plenty of questions. Healthcare professionals, while desiring to be personal in their healing, are overloaded with calls for attention and can easily project that they don't have the time needed to really talk with their patients. The loved ones and intimately involved caregivers may have the time, but are too tired. They've been monitoring care, signing forms, calling family members, and are frankly just too fatigued to deal with questions. Or they may be frightened of being drawn into the wilderness of dying, where the questions might have no easy answers. As pastors and leaders we often neglect a critical part of ministry with those who are dying. We are called to be catalysts, facilitators, and mediators for dialogue. Many of the questions will be medical decisions that often lead into serious moral or ethical reflection. Those questions will usually have some faith dimension to them. Whether it's the simple question of information about the next medical procedure or the more difficult decision of turning to palliative care, we may be asked to facilitate and even mediate a discussion among the parties who have an interest in the answer. Often these parties will gravitate together naturally for the discussion, but in cases of hesitancy we will be called to risk encouraging dialogue. Gaining the trust of nurses and doctors can allow us to play a vital role for families who are unschooled in the institutions where healthcare is provided. It is often true that the first line of knowledge is the nursing and patient-care support staff. It is helpful to nurture trusting relationships with nurses. Talking with them at their stations, recognizing their good work when they enter a room, bringing them candy or snacks—all these express appreciation and acknowledge their important roles. Asking for advice on how our ministry can be helpful, learning their names so we will be included as a part of the healing team will also strengthen our role as advocates for dialogue. We might also be facilitators in healing broken family relationships. We will become privy to long-harbored and possibly not-so-disguised feelings of separation and anger. Once a patient said to me, "I need all the prayers I can get to help refrain from killing some of my relatives before I breathe my last!" If the separated parties are in the healing room, asking them to help with patient-care needs might be the foundation for bridge building. Helping the patient to write a letter of grace and forgiveness, with or without delivery, can be cathartic. Through the use of humor we can become the lightning rod to deflect and dissipate the rancor among people. We may ask the sick or dying if they would like us to contact the person in the adversarial relationship in an attempt to begin the reconciliation process.

The phone rings and the voice says, "Charlie just died. What am I to do now?" These words are asking for answers about how a grieving family proceeds from this moment of death to the words of committal at the final resting place of a loved one's earthly body. It should be expected that we know all things funereal and all the nuances of ritual. We are to be there for the bereaved in dealing not only with the spiritual but also the earthly realities such as funeral expenses. Becoming a trusted but objective partner with those in the funeral industry is necessary. Having a serious working knowledge of the funeral homes and their personnel and practices is essential for good pastoral care of the grieving. From the time of death to the final farewell ritual, we should have an established and uniform procedure.

Before the call we can take these steps:

- Offer seminars on death-and-dying issues with clergy, funeral directors, estate planners, healthcare professionals.
- Open discussions on the theological and ethical issues surrounding dying and the terminal illness process. Make available advanced directives and legal information.
- List Internet resources and offer print materials.
- Make available and, if requested, file funeral arrangement preplanning booklets.
- Display pamphlets and brochures throughout the church that offer support for the time of illness and death.
- Preach sermons and have remembrance worship opportunities throughout the year—All Saints' Day, healing services, Good Friday, labyrinth walks focusing on healing and wholeness.
- Create handouts for planning a funeral or memorial service describing the church's philosophy on the funeral service, an order of a service, scripture selections, music, hymns, as well as guides for those who will speak and eulogize, and lists of fees for the church staff. This helps to keep our role focused on bereavement care rather than administrative issues.
- Prepare lay leadership to share the pastoral care and oversight of the funeral service—calling and caring, ushering, receptions.

At the time of the death we should do the following:

- Be present with the family or visit within a brief time after the death to support and to pray.
- Be a calming presence and a guide through the "What to do now?" period.

- Assist with contacting the healthcare professionals and the funeral director.
- Assist the funeral home personnel with informing the family when the body is being removed.
- Answer the faith, emotional, and practical questions as they arise.

Within thirty-six hours, make a second visit in order to:

- Continue to support the family in the grieving process.
- Begin planning the funeral service.
- Moderate the many voices of family members with multiple perspectives and help to keep the power in the hands of those closest to the deceased.
- Gather basic information to share—time, hour, other details—needed for the church to prepare for the service.

In visits to the funeral home, we should be:

- A familiar presence amid the unfamiliar.
- A discerning listener to the actual wishes of the deceased and the bereaved.
- A clarifier of information needed by the funeral director at a time when clarity of thought is tested by grief.
- A presence that is familiar with funeral rituals and practices—waiting periods, the ways of disposing of the body, container selection depending on the type of disposal, cemetery requirements, etc.
- A voice for the role of the church in all of this.

At calling or visitation hours, either at the funeral home, in the church, or on rare occasions in the family home, we should be:

- A presence to comfort during the family's initial viewing of the loved one's body.
- A prayerful presence.

- A clarifer of final details with the family and the funeral director about the funeral or memorial service.

At one funeral, the seventh eulogizer was fifteen minutes into his words of remembrance when a saintly spider triggered the fire alarm. After eight minutes, the chaos subsided. Believing that it was my time to move the service along I walked toward the pulpit. But no, the eulogizer continued for another nine minutes. The family was appalled. Following the service I was questioned, "What happened?" All I could say was, "You should have communicated my advice: 'Unless you are otherwise instructed, the family requests that you be sensitive to the length of your remarks.'" To the best of our abilities we are to oversee and coordinate the Christian funeral. This is one of the most difficult aspects of ministry. The reality is that emotion often far overrides reason in planning a funeral liturgy. While helping the family deal with their grief, their regrets, their unfinished business, their confusion, their relief, etc., in a gentle manner, we make it clear that when it comes to the celebration of the hope of resurrection we are the experts. In remembering the sacredness of one human life and the promise of eternal life, the supporting cast in the theater of the Spirit consists of funeral directors, close relatives and friends, and eulogizers. By our pastoral, professional demeanor and by providing information about the role of the church in a Christian funeral as described in the church's funeral materials, it should be clear who is in charge of working with the family in preparing the funeral liturgy.

In the planning of the service, several areas of the liturgy need our utmost attention:

- scripture readings
- speakers
- selection of music
- creation of the physical space
- the final interment

"Can we have the Psalm that talks about still waters in the service? You know Psalm . . . " I couldn't stand the person's pain as he struggled to save his reputation for biblical knowledge. “Twenty-three,” I said quietly. “Yes, that’s it! Mom always loved that passage of scripture. And my daughter has written a poem about her grandmother, so she can read that next. You know she adored her grandmother!” A familiar Psalm and a junior high schooler who wants to be the next Maya Angelou—that was the extent of the requests for grandma’s last farewell on earth. While this case is the exception to the rule, finding meaningful scripture for a funeral is becoming increasingly difficult. There are a growing number of unaffiliated Christians, and biblical literacy is not a high priority for them. Unless the family has had particular instruction from the deceased, or a family member has a favorite passage, we should take the lead on the selection of scripture. Other readings, such as poems by grandchildren or love sonnets by Shakespeare, should be read at the designated time for eulogizing and not as a partner with scripture. If necessary, additional brief writings and eulogies can be included as a bulletin insert or in a looseleaf notebook provided by the family or church. It may add work for the church secretary, but it brings more sanity and sanctity to the service.

If there is any area where a funeral service can lose its flow and where the worship leader can feel the most out of control, it is the time of eulogizing. Here are some suggestions for dealing with frustrated preachers and over-emotional speakers:

- Have the families agree on a time period for eulogizing of not more than twenty-five minutes. Then have them set the ground rules by which you can have some control.
- Offer the family an opportunity for the worship leader to review and assist the speakers in presenting a well-crafted eulogy.
- Place this portion of the service just before the benediction. Put a note in the order of worship: “If because of the length of the service and prior commitments you must leave early, please do so by the ____________ door.” If placed beneath the eulogies, this may prompt discretion from the speakers.
- Offer to blend into the homily the brief remarks from family and friends to help in keeping the speaker list brief.
- If all else fails, have the organist start to play.

Rob was a dear friend who died a tragic death: he lost a valiant fight with ALS. He was a percussionist in a rock band, and by the time of his death his hands were incapable of playing any of the more than one thousand percussion instruments he owned, not even his Peruvian goat toenails. As we planned his service, the question came up whether one of the most accomplished blues guitarists in the New England area could play at the service. My only response was that the music had to be discussed with the church's music director and we had to include hymns of celebration. I remember saying, "We are allowed to feel blue but resurrection must be announced!" A ten-minute blues version of "Amazing Grace" brought tears of sorrow and smiles of remembrance. Just before the final benediction, a recording of the only song Rob had ever sung publicly was played, "Drift Away." "Thanks for the joy you've given me. . . . You've helped me get along, making me strong. . . . Give me the beat, boys, and free my soul. . . ." The benediction said, "God's melody in Jesus Christ gave Rob the beat that freed his soul, and now he joyously has drifted into God's eternal care." This was the prelude for a New Orleans–style "When the Saints Go Marching In," which sent Rob's spirit on its way to eternity.

Tom was a committed church member, and, next to Jesus and family, his great love was the Chicago Cubs. Yes, he was a patient and long-suffering man. Since his family was going to find *some* way to have some of his ashes end up on Wrigley Field, his daughter asked if our organist would play "Take Me Out to the Ball Game." Let us just say, with his Cubs hat on and after we sang "For All the Saints," he left the church in style for those extra innings that have been promised in the Gospel. And oh, yes, when a double was hit to right field and all eyes were on the fielder, some of his ashes just happened to float from the left field stands at the historic ballpark.

Music selection for funerals should also take the following into account:

- *Christian hymns*: For music at a funeral, hymns are the primary resource. Favorite hymns can be used in preludes and postludes and for congregational singing. Additionally, secular music that has very inspiring lyrics can be appropriate and fit comfortably with the Good News of the Gospel. Some contemporary composers have the gift of weaving musical notes together that calm the soul or celebrate the gift of life. During the meditative moments, such compositions can be woven into the service and used without the lyrics.

- *Appropriate secular music:* A solo sung by a relative in preparation during the prelude could be fine, or a song could be sung once the final benediction is given, either as the casket is removed from the sanctuary or as people sit in remembrance prior to the postlude. Some secular music might also fit comfortably into the selection for the postlude.
- *The musician and the musical instruments:* Having the church's director of music or organist be a part of the liturgical planning is essential. It's not wise to overlook the musicians' skill level and the capabilities of the church's keyboard instruments. Since music is an essential resource for the worship of God, it needs to be presented with integrity for both remembrance of the deceased's life and the church's theology.

When the service is held in the church sanctuary there are preparations for how the space will be used. In addition to the casket or container for ashes, flowers and personal memorabilia may be added to the worship space. It is a good practice to have a sanctuary plan available for funeral directors and families. The symbols of the church—baptismal fonts, Communion tables, altars, crosses—should be off-limits for the placement of anything except flowers. Particularly in the case of cremations or the absence of the body, a photo of the deceased on a table in the front of the sanctuary could be considered. All other collages or pieces of memorabilia could be displayed in entranceways to the sanctuary and in proximity to the receiving line. The church's symbols that announce resurrection and eternal life should be clearly in evidence.

Carrying a Casket

I had tried to be a helpful presence. In was a snowy, blustery winter's day. The family had rushed to their cars and the casket

> was sitting in the church narthex with only three funeral home personnel to carry it to the hearse. So I volunteered. As we hoisted the casket into the hearse I heard a ripping sound. As the wind blew and I felt suddenly cooler, I realized the seam on my trousers had ripped. Off to the hilltop cemetery we went. I again helped to carry the casket to the grave, with a black raincoat covering the clothing malfunction. The family had pulled their car close to the grave and had opened the window just a crack so they could hear the words of committal. The preacher freezing in the snow, the family feeling the warmth of God's love within their car—the committal service went on unabbreviated. The dead deserve it.

Whether we are at a snowy grave just before the casket is lowered into the ground or on a boat about to scatter ashes at sea, our presence can do many things:

- It can offer a respectful and hopeful moment of closure.
- It can provide arms and a shoulder to hold on to.
- It can assist the funeral director in dealing with the emotions of the bereaved.

From the first call announcing a death, to the body's final resting place, our presence provides the mourners with hope and support and leaves us with a sense that our ministry matters.

Once again a respected friend, the nationally awarded writer and funeral director Thomas Lynch, underscores the importance of our task as the overseer of this rite of passage.

> The dead, of course, do not much care. They are predictably indifferent to such details. Perhaps it is the first gift of paradise. The dead don't care. Only the living do. Whether faith furnishes our heavens, or doubt leaves the decor up for grabs, or wonder keeps the particulars ever changing, Whoever is in Charge there must take care of them. . . .
>
> We do what we do for the living's sake. The living must decide when the time has come to cease looking and begin

> to mourn, to organize the liturgies of thanks and praise and affliction, to shake a fist in God's face and say the ancient prayers. All the dead require is witness and remembrance—to say they lived, they died, they matter to us.[3]

It is our awesome responsibility to help the living decide how to memorialize and remember the dead and to proclaim the hope that faith offers. It is also our call to give meaning to the life of the person between the dates on the headstone. The rest is in the hands of our gracious, life-affirming God. It is God who has written a comma at the end of the sentence about life that means there is more to come.

The funeral has ended and for some of the bereaved the darkness of grief will subside quickly. The most bereaved will feel lost or even abandoned. All of us have heard the words of those who are left to reshape their lives after the death of a loved one. Two of the most striking and insightful attempts at expressing the feeling of loss I have heard were spoken several months after the funeral, when most of the supportive family and friends had returned to their regular routines.

- "My crutches have all gone away. It is difficult to walk lame."
- "I am living in a land where everyone is speaking English, but it all sounds like a foreign language to me."

The crutches do go away. Family and cherished friends will be less attentive because they have their own lives to live. The truth also is that those walking lame will often be so introspective about shattered hopes, unfinished business, unresolved hurts, and blessed memories that the words of support offered will be almost unintelligible. During this time of walking lame and being disconnected, we, as pastors and church leaders, take on one of our more crucial roles. We become a shoulder to lean on and an interpreter for the person as he or she walks through a foreign land. In this new partnership we must help the bereaved remember responsibly, reconnect, and refocus.

The word "responsibly" when wedded with remembering seems unduly harsh following a loved one's death. But prolonged deep grieving is harmful to the person's well-being and often drives away caring people who sincerely want to comfort. One unique way of remembering is to journal. We can help the bereaved to compose a narrative or poem about their journey through grief. This could be added to an ever-expanding devotional booklet to be passed on to others who are facing such sorrow. The encouragement of some tangible memorializing of the loved one—a gift to support a mission outreach, gifts of tangible items needed by the church or another service organization, a scholarship for an in-need youth, anything that might benefit others and have a connection to the loved one's life—is yet another avenue for remembrance. Through the church's ministries or through helping to establish several formal times of remembrance throughout the year, a leader may help the bereaved to set aside the daily recurring cycle of pain. Monthly healing services, All Saints' Day remembrances, an anniversary service in the home—these can foster responsible remembering.

The church has been a pioneer in the ministry of reconnecting for the bereaved. From support groups to individual visitations, the church has designed numerous opportunities for reconnecting. Knowing the survivors' gifts and talents allows the church to invite the bereaved to use those gifts in ministry. Imagine recently widowed members of the church as caretakers in the church school nursery. It has happened. Imagine the pairing in a service project of teenagers with those who have experienced recent loss. Naturally our main way of encouraging reconnection is a plan to systematically contact the person during the first year following the loss. With the gift of technology, we can be reminded of those times and make meaningful personal contact. The church should be a force in the process of reconnection.

There comes a time in the grieving process when refocusing is essential for mental and physical health. There comes a time when we all must walk lame. We might be called to a role as supportive presence and objective companion in this refocusing journey. From issues as mundane as helping to make decisions on the disposal of a loved one's clothing to where to sit in church to issues of living arrangements—all may become part of our continuing pastoral care. Keeping lists of worthy organizations to receive used clothing as well as youth or others to assist in delivering the clothing might become part of our ministry. Encouraging friends to sit with the person in worship is one small way to refocus. How about asking, "What would [*name of the loved one*] want you to do?" In some cases it's useful to know a human resources professional from the church community who will offer time and expertise about reentering the job market. Financially astute church members who can keep confidences could be made available to assist in understanding the new financial realities.

At the time of death and dying, the church is invited in, and since we are in the shalom business, the bringing of spiritual, physical, and emotional wholeness, our care should be compassionate and comprehensive. But then this is universally true for all three of these ministries of hatching, matching, and dispatching. We are invited to be a blessing, and the resources of the community of faith are being sought. It is a privilege yet an awesome responsibility.

Inspiration

For everything there is a season,
and a time for every matter under heaven:
a time to be born, and a time to die; . . .
a time to weep, and a time to laugh;
a time to mourn, and a time to dance. (Eccl 3:1-6)

Prayer

God who blessed the little children, who brought the good wine to a marriage at Cana, and who called Lazarus to rise, we thank you for allowing us entrance into the most sacred moments in people's lives. May our presence bring a blessing into these holy times. Through our silence, our words, our attentive spirit may your compassion and love touch the hearts of those who ask us to enter into the most sacred passages of their lives. Amen.

8

Putting the Awe and Aha into the Theater of the Spirit

Worship That Inspires and Transforms

Body Building Exercises

- Why do we worship? What is the most important part of the worship liturgy?
- What is the role of the worship leader in this ministry?
- What is the role of the worshipper?
- Reflect on one of the most meaningful worship services in which you participated. Why was it so meaningful?

In all humility, it was an inspiring worship service! The music was uplifting. The moments of silence were artfully timed to allow for a spirit of solitude to embrace the soul. A scripture passage was read with a storyteller's simplicity by the lay reader. And the sermon—I shall set modesty aside—seemed to offer each worshipper a word of hope and joy to carry with them. We have all had those days when we felt an overpowering presence of God's Spirit in worship. The last person in a lengthy line streaming from the sanctuary was the senior deacon, a rather nattily attired septuagenarian who had the art of seating people so that the six-hundred-seat sanctuary would seem comfortably full regardless of the attendance, greeted me energetically, "This is God's day, so rejoice and be glad in it!" Nathaniel, a Yale graduate, always tried to find a positive word to say as he left the sanctuary: "Great show! If you keep this up the ticket sales will increase!" As the renewal of the church progressed, I heard "Great shows!" over and over. But with this continual repetition, I found myself wanting to say, "This isn't a show.

It's worship. And furthermore, I was not offering a dramatic reading, I was laying out the comfort and challenge of the Gospel and . . . my guts up there!"

"Great show!" Those words always haunted me until I heard someone refer to worship as the theater of the Spirit. That image of worship resonated with me and what I had always meant it to be. One of the early definitions for the word "theater" seemed very appropriate for worship: "Open-air place in ancient times for viewing spectacles." While we typically think of theaters being enclosed space, our worship, regardless of its enclosure, should allow the winds of the Spirit to blow away the dust and dirt from our lives. It should refresh the worshippers for their life journeys. During initial research on the concept of theater, I was reminded of the theater of the absurd. This is a theatrical form in which much that appears rational by worldly standards is set aside and new ways of looking at reality are woven into the play. What a remarkable definition when applied to worship! It is only by faith in the Incarnate God, not the rational world, that we can make sense of life and we can learn to live victoriously. Paul's words to the church at Corinth give validation to seeing worship as the theater of the absurd: "but we proclaim Christ crucified, a stumbling-block to Jews and foolishness to Gentiles" (1 Cor 1:23). Paul continues by proclaiming that the message of the Gospel is foolishness to those who have bought into the "rational" world's way of thinking. To Paul's words many would say, "That's absurd!"

The concept of worship as theater of the Spirit with a dose of the theater of the absurd blended in could be a reenergizing approach to planning and leading worship. Because of the fine line between show and theater of the Spirit we approach the creation and implementation of the liturgy prayerfully. The fine line between worship being a human show or being theater of the Spirit is fine indeed. In our preparation and implementation of worship, we must wrestle with this reality that worship is to be about the Holy One and not us. The main difference is that our script is built on the foundation of the Gospel of Jesus Christ.

Another basic understanding of the essence of worship comes from Danish philosopher and theologian Søren Kierkegaard. He felt that most Christians defined worship in the following theatrical terms: God was the prompter for the preacher, who was the actor, with the congregation being the audience. Kierkegaard countered with a most provocative notion: The preacher is the prompter, the worshippers are the actors, and God is the audience. With these concepts of the theater of the Spirit and Kierkegaard's imagery in mind, the planning and oversight of worship becomes a more daunting task.

The prayerful and creative approach to planning and leading worship is primary in building and retaining a vital church. Gathered worship is where people are usually first introduced to the Gospel and to a particular congregation. It is the place where all meet and greet; that is, as equal, regardless of their station in life. It is the place where people can entertain God with their praise and leave with the idea of entertaining the Gospel message in their daily lives.

These theatrical images lead to a fresh understanding of two roles for those who are responsible to lead the worship of their church. The roles are

- Producer-Director
- Prompter

The Producer-Director

In theater, the producer is the person who brings together all of the elements required for the success of the theatrical performance. The producer draws together the needed resources to get the show off the ground. The director coordinates the resources—script, actors, musicians, lighting, and audio professionals—to bring the production to performance.

The Prompter

The prompters help the actors remember their lines. They stand in the wings ready to assist the performers to play out their roles to the best of their abilities.

If taken seriously, these two theater-based roles can be the catalysts for transforming worship. We need to also be reminded that possibly the most significant time in our worship ministry starts before show time.

In the theater of the Spirit, the acts in the drama have traditionally been praise, confession, proclamation, and dedication. These are sound pillars on which to build the worship service. The outcomes of these acts should be *awe, aha,* and *action.* A time of gathered worship should bring awe: a feeling of mystery and majesty that leads to praise of God and the humble acknowledgment that we are not God. Worship should lead to aha moments: times of insight and renewal of spirit and mind. It should also be a catalyst for action: going into the world and carrying out acts of grace and justice.

All Worshippers Are Not Alike

In the initial planning stage of worship, there is one element often forgotten: no two worshippers (actors) are alike. Personality types differ; life experiences vary, and personal tastes fluctuate; cultural, racial, and ethnic backgrounds are diverse. So how is one to plan a worship service that will engage the worshippers' active participation in the drama? Some want the brass-band worship with its majesty and pomp. Others want to hear the still small voice of God in silent meditative reflection. This diversity adds a further dimension to the task of planning worship. Some larger churches will seek to overcome this challenge with multiple services. But many churches would find it difficult to offer that option.

So we must keep diversity in mind while producing and directing worship. Times need to be woven in for extroverted praise, meditative silence, community interaction, and hopeful dreaming. While designing the service it is helpful to visualize the worshipping congregation. Is there something in the service that will draw in the many different personality types and life situations that will be in the worshipping community? We must responsibly set aside our personal preferences in the planning of worship.

As I was standing in the welcoming line one time after worship, I was greeted by a woman who had the look of joy and contentment on her face. I was touched to think my sermon had spoken so deeply to her need. Her words were measured and filled with emotion. "I can't thank you enough . . ." She paused to gather herself so she could offer the appropriate words to express her appreciation for what I thought was my sermon. "I can't thank you enough for the lengthy silence at the time of the pastoral prayer. You are one of the few pastors I know who allows more than a minute for me to center myself in the Spirit." Being an extrovert by nature and concerned about the service taking more than an hour, I find the final fifteen seconds of silent prayer excruciating. But for my more pensive, introverted parishioner, silence is the moment when the veil between earth and heaven is lifted. The producer of worship clearly needs to be attentive to the diversity of the worshipping community.

Remember: There Are Five Senses

We also do well to remember that the five senses should be taken into account in planning for worship. What is being seen? How is the sense of hearing being called on? Are there ways that the tactile sense can be more fully involved? How could the senses of taste and smell be more fully integrated to enhance the relationship with God and one another? Actually, church worship has subtly used the senses throughout its history. Visual symbols, spoken words, and music (chanted or sung or instrumental), incense, bread and wine, passing the peace—the senses have brought spiritual depth and meaning to worship. Too often worship becomes largely an audiovisual event. In an effort to make worship more fully sensorial I have dusted Christmas bulletins with baby powder to remind the worshippers of the innocent power of the birthing day; thrown water from pine branches as a remembrance of baptism vows; mixed vinegar with the communion wine on Good Friday as a remembrance of the bitter sweet message of Holy Week; given congregants lumps of clay to feel or mold during a sermon on the potter and the clay; projected a night sky onto the dome of the sanctuary and invoked a time of total silence as a reminder of the shepherds' experience while tending their flocks. The creative uses of the sensorial are limitless. The worship planner needs to be sure that worship is more than merely a two-sense experience.

The producer-director in the planning of the drama needs to be keenly aware of these:

- The place and space of worship
- The physical blocking of worship

The building's architecture, the sanctuary floor plan, the lighting, the symbols that are part of the interior design, the mobility of seating, and the other large worship resources (altars, pulpits, etc.) need to be considered in planning worship. Whether serving in large gothic cathedrals or New England–style white clapboard meetinghouses, I can attest that architecture and space do make a theological statement. The awe and mystery of the Holy can be felt in a cathedral setting; the feeling of Christian community is more easily experienced in the brightly lighted, open feeling of clear-windowed meetinghouses. The producer-director needs to consider the following questions when planning for the use of the worship space:

- How can the seating be arranged (movable chairs) or how can I best use the pews to give focus to the theme of worship?
- How and where should I place the worship resources to create the visual message that complements the focus of the text's theme for the morning?
- What spirit or thought provoking objects can I strategically locate in the worship space?

Seating makes a statement. Eyes forward or people facing other worshippers, a shoulder-to-shoulder or more open configuration—important unspoken messages are given in the seating configuration. This is especially true in large-building churches with a small membership, where large empty gaps can project messages of distance, aloofness, and coldness. With modest resistance—by those who have *their* seats—the roping off of pews or the elimination of chairs can give the space a feeling of vitality and warmth.

Where to place the altar or the baptismal font or bowl? Pulpit or no pulpit? Where to have the choir seated? Where to place religious symbols, banners, even the cross? These simple questions, if answered creatively, can provide depth to the witness of the Gospel. Suppose the cross was missing and no one realized it. What a subtle sermon could be preached on the meaning of the cross. The decision on whether to place the altar or Communion table elevated in the chancel area of the sanctuary or on the same level as the people offers very different understandings of the Eucharist. Consider the removal of all the furnishings so that a play or dance can give greater meaning to the scripture.

When seeking a moment of awe or aha, the inclusion of unusual, thought-provoking objects in the worship space will raise eternal questions without a word being spoken. Why are Dali paintings or church-member family photos being displayed on easels throughout the sanctuary? Why are there a dozen colored eggs on the Communion table? Why is an unkempt stranger sitting in my pew? Why is there a dove in a large birdcage beside the pulpit? Why is there a safari hat on the altar? What is that children's toy circus tent, with animals, doing on a table in the middle of the center aisle? Did the custodian forget the mop on the side of the chancel? Why is that "curve in road ahead" sign at the entrance to the sanctuary? What does it mean that there is an Indiana Jones movie running in the fellowship hall as we enter worship? Appropriately placed objects can spawn questions and thoughts in the worshipper that will increase the depth of participation in the worship service.

It is helpful for the producer-director to obtain or create a planning tool in which all of the elements of worship are addressed. For one example of such a tool, see Appendix B, Worship Planning Funnel. This and other similar resources will encourage initial brainstorming before sermon details and worship order are finalized. After the funnel, as I call it, is filled with everything from random one-liners or life stories or references from the arts and exegetical information based on respected scholarship, then a prayerful distillation of all of the thoughts can take place. This distillation usually will prompt a theme or direction for the worship service. Then a selection of the worship resources can be completed to complement the underlying focus of the service. The brainstorming part of planning can include laity and staff colleagues. Such preplanning is essential for a worship experience that is cohesive and inspiring.

At this point an important reality of church life and its effect on worship planning needs to be addressed. Smaller-membership churches (often defined as under two hundred members) are in the majority in many denominations. Often their leadership, when planning worship, is drawn to a large-church model. This mind-set can have less-than-successful consequences. It often manifests itself most vividly in the music selection and the instrument on which it is played. In my judicatory ministry, I have attended and led worship at dozens of these small but mighty families of faith. I have heard five-voice choirs struggling to sing a classic oratorical work. I have listened to organ selections written for large multimanual cathedral organs played painfully on ancient poor-quality organs. Two-part singing of historic and contemporary hymns by the choir is a pleasing alternative to the presentation of more difficult choral pieces by a small choir with few sight-readers. In smaller-membership churches hymnals can become a primary resource for the selection of choral music. Using individuals with musical talent on a monthly or bimonthly basis can enhance the music ministry and give the choir more time to prepare for their choral presentation. In some musically challenged church settings, even a cappella singing or recorded music or music prerecorded into an electronic keyboard should be considered. In planning for worship in the small-church setting, the propensity to attempt to mimic the larger church worship experience should be handled carefully.

While in the Protestant tradition the sermon has often been given center stage, other areas are given less attention in the worship planning process. Relegating them to a secondary position in worship can lead to:

- uncoordinated music
- stagnant (dull, lifeless) scripture reading
- preachy prayers
- nonchalant sacraments

Uncoordinated Music—Finding Peace with the War Department

Some clergy consider the music department to be "the war department." This designation is occasionally accurate because musicians can be rigid in their understanding of what is good and appropriate church music. Some who have been in their positions for a long period of time have built an ally base. In smaller-membership churches the pool of musical talent can be quite limited, and highly trained professional musicians may be difficult to procure. So the direct involvement by the producer-director of worship is imperative. Dynamic worship requires respect and humility between clergy and the music team. A healthy relationship can add a depth to worship that is unattainable if mutual respect is lacking. Open and honest dialogue that fosters profound creativity and honest disagreement needs to be established in the clergy-musician relationship. Along with mutual respect, the following understandings are needed:

- In roadblock situations the pastor or leader makes the final call. When a musician has been on staff before the new minister, clarity about roles in the leadership of worship needs to be established with the lay church leaders before accepting a call.
- The role of music in worship is not to elevate the tastes of the worshippers, but to provide them with music in their own vernacular that gives voice to their desire to praise God. Because of the diversity in the congregation, diversity of the best of historic and contemporary church music needs to be included in the liturgy.
- Both the minister and the musician need to publicly affirm their mutual respect. This will include a spiritual dimension in their relationship. Through prayer and scripture both need to be reminded that it is not about either of them.

While there have been some moments in my ministry when I strongly disagreed with the music staff, in general I feel that I have been blessed with colleagues whose knowledge of the broad corpus of church music and their instrumental and choral directing gifts have complemented my efforts to bring the Word alive in worship. Along with the historic music of the Christian church, several on my music staff have significantly helped in efforts to include jazz, big band, rock, Gospel and other genres of music: Going for Baroque; the Gospel according to Dr. Seuss or James Taylor; Jesus on Broadway; Getting a Handle on Handel, Anyone? An atmosphere of mutual respect and a commitment to speaking the truth in love between clergy and music staff can bring the Gospel alive with greater energy than merely the spoken word. The war department can become the joy and peace department. Strong alliances can lead to Spirit-filled, energized worship.

A Crowded Manger—This is the Word of God—Stagnant Scripture Reading

I always anticipate Christmas Eve readings of the passage in Luke that speaks of the arrival of the shepherds. I call it the "How many were in the manger?" passage (Lk 2:16). If you read the passage without previous study, you will often find two adults and one baby lying in the manger. Remember the shepherds' arrival: "And they came with haste and found Mary and Joseph and the babe lying in a manger" (KJV). I have typed it without punctuation because it is often read as if there are no commas. I would estimate half of all Christmas Eve readers are guilty of the no-comma reading. With commas, we are told that Mary and Joseph are present in the scene and that a baby is lying alone in the manger. "And they came with haste, and found Mary, and Joseph, and the babe lying in a manger." Not so crowded now!

"This is the Word of the Triune God." "Thanks be to God." are often the closing words spoken at the conclusion of the reading of the scripture lessons. "This is the Word of the Lord!" That sounds like the reading of scripture should be taken with utter seriousness. Preparation for the reading of the Word should not be rushed. We need to remember the differing writing styles found in the Bible. There are story-like narratives about the children of Israel and Jesus' life and teachings. There is wisdom literature and prophetic cries that are poetic and prosaic. There are letters that carry with them the full gamut of emotions. Each requires a different sensitivity to pace in its reading. We also have the eternal struggle of how to coalesce seamlessly ancient literary and cultural contexts with contemporary thought and lifestyles. The abundance of Bible translations adds a further challenge for the public reading of scripture. There was a saintly woman who faithfully attended weekly Bible study. Most of the attendees had the New Revised Standard Version, the King James Version, or the New King James Version. Moffatt was her translation. It was the group's practice to share in the reading of the texts. When Saint Ellie, as I called her, volunteered to read, most of the group would take on a puzzled look as they tried to follow along. The words often sounded awkward and odd. Ellie loved her Moffatt translation. The inquisitive looks came from the fact that James Moffat was a Scottish theologian and professor who in his translation used words and phrases that would be familiar to an early-twentieth-century student in Glasgow, Scotland. Translation selection is a dicey task when reading scripture in public.

Those who read scripture need to make the necessary preparation so the drama and message of the text is not lost. Often scripture is assigned to lay readers. We should applaud efforts at lay participation, but be concerned unless training in the art of reading scripture is first conducted. Without such training we are doing a disservice to the proclamation of the Gospel. One of my first lay readers who made the Word come alive would often say to me, "It was that elocution class at Yale that provided me with my abilities in reading scripture." After he read the Good Friday narrative of the final hours of Jesus' life and several worshippers were on the verge of tears he whispered to me "I wish I had the Kleenex concession." Training matters. Here are some points for the preparation for reading scripture:

- *No dumb reading*. In the United Church of Christ heritage, the historical practice in Pilgrim or Puritan worship was to set the text in context before reading the lesson. Otherwise it was called dumb reading. A brief few lines to set the context helps the hearer become engaged with the text. Here, too, a knowledge of basic textual research tools is essential. Occasionally the inclusion of several thought-provoking questions can draw the listener in. If you were Jesus, what would you have done? If you were to preach on this lesson, what would be the theme of your sermon?

- *Punctuation always counts.* The text requires good public speaking and dramatic skills. While a reader may be awed by the text, there is no place for the side effects of visible nervousness—rushed, whispered, or shouted reading. It is often helpful to mark the text with a highlighter and with comments in the margins.
- *Vary the forms of delivery.* Many texts are ripe for dramatic reading by more than one person. The use of other staff members or trained lay persons can bring the text to life. The lesson becomes audiovisual. Many texts lend themselves to congregational responsive reading.

Scripture is not meant to complement the sermon. Rather the sermon is to complement scripture. Preworship preparation is vital.

Hear Us P-R-A-Y !—Preachy Prayers

His voice was usually warm and welcoming. His soothing tone drew you in to listen more closely to his words. But when he offered the pastoral prayer in worship, his voice became ominous and stiff: "HOLY GOD, YOU WHO ARE CREATOR AND SUSTAINER. . . ." Often the prayer was a summation of the sermon themes: "AND REMIND US LIKE THE PRODIGAL SON THAT WE ARE IN NEED OF YOUR GRACE, AND WE ASK THAT YOU WILL BRING US TO OUR SENSES SO THAT WE WILL COME HOME TO YOUR ENFOLDING ARMS." The length of his prayers was an interminable four or five minutes. His prayers were more dramatic public orations than heart-felt dialogues with God. They did little to remove the veil between God and the worshippers.

Public prayer is not easy. It is meant to help center the worshippers so that they may be drawn into their own prayers of praise, confession, and intercession. The pastoral prayers of the community should be the catalysts for each worshipper to offer her or his own personal prayers to God and then have a moment to listen for the Spirit's still small voice.

Father Anthony de Mello was a spiritual guide for those seeking to understand a life of prayer and meditation. In his book *Taking Flight,*[1] he offers the following story about a poor farmer:

> Late one evening a poor farmer on his way back from the market found himself without his prayer book. The wheel of his cart had come off right in the middle of the woods and it distressed him that this day should pass without his having said his prayers.
>
> So this is the prayer he made: "I have done something very foolish, Lord. I came away from home this morning without my prayer book and my memory is such that I cannot recite a single prayer without it. So this is what I am going to do: I shall recite the alphabet five times very slowly and you, to whom all prayers are known, can put the letters together to form the prayers I can't remember."
>
> And the Lord said to his angels, "Of all the prayers I have heard today, this one was undoubtedly the best because it came from a heart that was simple and sincere."

Our role in leading public prayer is to offer the alphabet so all may encounter God's presence.

Public prayer can take many forms. Again, as with scripture, preparation is essential, even for extemporaneous prayer. The formation of a prayer begins with the needs of the community and the wider world. The joys and concerns of the congregation and the needs of the world are the catalyst for meaningful prayer. Even with all the words we speak, the pastoral prayer is primarily for listening for God's whispering voice. Our words only prepare us for the essence of real prayer. I have always been moved by the prayers of my good friend Dr. Ted Loder. He has spoken of the time he spends each week in preparing the pastoral prayer. His words are simple, yet eloquent. This prayer offers that essence of what the worshipper should experience when the pastoral prayer is offered:

> O Holy One, I hear and say many words,
> Yet yours is the Word I need.
> Speak now, and help me to listen,
> And if what I hear is silence, let it quiet me,
> Let it disturb me, let it touch my need,
> Let it break my pride, let it shrink my certainties.[2]

Varying the forms and types of prayers can give energy to public prayer.

- *Extemporaneous Prayer:* requires focusing on the moment and the concerns of the people now. It usually requires a slower paced presentation so that the Spirit can help to shape the flow. A few key words , written down, can help avoid rambling prayers.
- *Written Prayer:* includes key words or phrases that serve as catalysts so the worshippers can enter into the prayer. These will provide the avenue for a more ordered prayer into which the elements of praise, confession, and intercession can be woven. Warning: while creative writing is an asset to prayer, artful poetry and eloquent prose can prove a distraction from soul-filled prayer.
- *Prayers written by others:* often guarantee a well-articulated prayer. If it comes from a denominational book of worship, it avoids the heresy of poor prayer theology. Many of the written or online prayer resources do not require an acknowledgment. However, an occasional reference such as "I am using a prayer by ______________________ because it seems so appropriate" is an act of grace. These prayers can be used as starting points for writing pastoral prayers. When using these prayers, take time to become familiar with them as if they were your own.
- *Guided Prayer:* invites the person to take a journey into scripture through questions that lead to personal reflection. Prayer mood-setting words that can work to center people and help them let go of those things that are blocking their connecting with the Spirit are liberating. This includes breath prayers and body prayers. There are dozens of guided prayer models available for use.
- *Silence:* allows many people to attentively listen for the breath of God. This is a prayer form often forgotten because of the constant cacophany of our world. Even when spoken prayers are offered, a significant time of silence at the time of the pastoral prayer—one minute or more—is appreciated by many.

The words of Mahatma Gandhi about prayer should cause us all to pause in the preparation of the pastoral prayer. "Prayer is not asking.

It is a longing of the soul. It is daily admission of one's weakness. It is better in prayer to have a heart without words than words without a heart."[3]

No German Beer-Hall Approach, Please—Nonchalant Sacraments

My wife has always been a source of honest critique of my ministry. Her direct assessment of my ministry gifts has humbled me when I most needed it. Early on in my ministry I received a word of advice about my administration of the sacraments. As we did our Sunday review of the worship service she mentioned the sacrament of the Lord's Supper—Communion, Eucharist, call it what you will. She thought my handling of the Communion chalice was a little too casual. "I know you were trying to make the cup seem accessible to everyone. But the way you swung it from side to side made me think you were in a German beer hall with a Bavarian band playing in the background. You were too nonchalant with the cup." It was then again that I was reminded that my administration of the sacraments required my utmost attention. The symbolic acts of baptism and communion carry deep truths with them. I needed to remember that they open the door to understandings of cleansing and redemption and renewal and sacrifice and community that go beyond any words we can speak. As worship leaders we need, to use a theater term, to "block" the movements and actions and to speak the liturgical language, in whatever form it is, in ways that are not rote but revealing of the mystery and simplicity inherent in the sacraments.

Whether the words come from the historic liturgies of the church or new contemporary ones, they need to be read as if it were for the very first time. They need to be shaped by the setting. I always faced a dilemma at the midnight Christmas Eve service when the Eucharist was celebrated at the time of a birth of the One who was to come in the name of God. Death. Birth. It seemed so incongruous. The words of invitation to the meal needed to fit the context: "this is the joyful feast of the people of God" or "this is the feast that offers us the nourishment required for rebirth." Since the sacraments are foundational liturgical acts, we must make every attempt to keep them meaningful and fresh when they are celebrated.

The sacraments are visual, and the blocking of them is important. Baptism is built on the concepts of cleansing, rebirth, remembrance, and incorporation into the family of God. Symbolic actions can help to draw out these concepts. Consider some of the options in officiating at the time of the sacraments:

- Pour the water into the bowl or font from a height that fills the worship space with the sound of cascading water.
- Place a few drops of Jordan River water into the bowl. Yes, it can be bought without paying for a trip to the Holy Land .
- Have the godparents or sponsors hold the bowl so they see they are making a commitment themselves to helping in nurturing the faith of the child.
- Walk into the congregation with the baby in our arms as a symbol of the congregation's nurturing responsibility and the child's inclusion into the church family.
- Present the parents or the baptized with the baptism bowl. It has become my practice to have the bowls designed and fired by at-risk youth potters from a local nonprofit organization. They become reminders that "I am baptized."
- Use shells, pine branches, or other natural objects to administer the water.
- If possible, move the baptismal bowl or font into the middle of the sanctuary.
- Have a moment of quiet reflection as all present think of their own baptisms.
- Encourage parents to talk with their child or children after church about the children's own baptisms.
- Encourage the inclusion of appropriate family traditions within the administration of the sacrament.

These suggestions will hopefully spawn other creative, not theatrical, ways of making sacred what some consider the "getting it done" moment.

While some may firmly believe there should be stringent requirements for baptism, the following are the basic expectations for the administration of the sacrament of baptism:

- There should first be a session with the parents or the individual. If the person is not a church member, future membership should be strongly considered. If the individual or child does not live in the area, a letter containing the baptismal record information could be forwarded to a church in the area where they live. The family must agree to welcoming a contact from that church.
- Regardless of where the baptism takes place, but preferably during worship, several members of the church must be in attendance to symbolize the community nature of the sacrament.
- And a most important consideration: no flash photography or hovering over the family for photo ops. Offering to remain after the service for pictures can help ease the frenetic picture-taking that detracts from the solemnity of the baptism. A correlative to this is that family and friends should remain for the entirety of the worship. Except for those attending to an infant or child's needs, which may require separate space to feed or calm the child, their understanding of the profound nature of the sacrament requires their full participation in worship.

As alluded to previously, Communion also requires extra attention to the message the visuals transmit. In places where there is a freestanding altar or table, the question needs to be asked, "Where should it be placed?" Placing it in an elevated chancel area suggests the mystery of the meal. Placed on the same level as the congregation suggests the humanity of Christ and that this is the family meal. Who will bake the bread or what kind of bread will be used? If church families are asked to bake the bread, should we provide a devotional resource for the time of baking the bread? If we wish to emphasize the global nature of the church, would it be appropriate to use a variety of ethnic breads on the table for sharing? Does a particular type of service lend itself better to altar, pew, or intinction Communion? What music shall be played or sung that will not interfere with the Spirit speaking during this sacred act? Might we include chalices made by potters in the congregation or glasses that hold special meaning from parishioners' homes?

A German beer-hall moment, a lifeless sprinkling of water, a rote act—or a life-giving moment? Nonchalance is not an option.

Children in Worship

"The Cat in the Hat told the Grinch that it is all in the Book, if you take time to look in the Book. . . ." These are the opening words of a sermon written for children of all ages. That's right: for toddlers and toddling seniors, for teenagers and mid-lifers. It was a sermon that used three familiar scripture lessons to tell the old, old story of the Big Who (God) and the Big Who Two (Jesus) and their love for all the world.

"Where's the picture of the church on the bulletin cover? Look at this stick-figure drawing of the Nativity. What might visitors to the church think of us? Why do you change things like this?" The forthright response was, "That looks like a masterpiece to the three-year-old artist and his parents."

No thorough look at worship can be written that does not include thoughts on children in worship. Done with clear intentions and planning, it can lead to moments of the truest worship of God that we can have. Done poorly, it can be blatant abuse, of using children for entertainment purposes.

I choose to use the words "Children in Worship" rather than "The Children's Sermon or Meditation." When children are in worship, the planner needs to be concerned about significant parts of liturgy being accessible to a child's mind and spirit. The selection of hymns, the framing of prayers, the administration of the sacraments and other parts of the worship service require exact planning so that children can participate as fully as adults.

The reason for children being in worship is not to learn patience through boredom, but rather to experience the presence of God and to learn how to respond to God's gracious love. Whether a church has weekly family worship or selected times for children to remain in the service, planning the liturgy when children are present needs to include looking at its flow through the eyes of a child.

The 4:30 p.m. Christmas Eve service was billed as the family service. An exceptionally trained and talented forty-voice youth choir gave primary leadership to the service. For three-quarters of the service, scripture lessons were read and traditional Christmas anthems and carols were sung, primarily by the choir. Near the end of the service, the plan had been for families to bring forward to an empty large crèche figures of cows and sheep and shepherds and magi and Mary and Joseph and the Babe. But by the time this family-friendly part of the service arrived, little children would be talking out loud, crying, walking across the pews, dancing in the aisles, and running out of crayons with which to color any white space on the worship program. The choir might sing majestically amid the reigning chaos, but what sense would it make to have an adult service sung by children? What we needed were life-size animated puppets! Isn't that what any church would do? A group of church artists gathered and created five-foot-high puppets of every character in the Nativity scene. With the help of a person with a knowledge of puppet making, arms were made to move and bodies were able to bow. The result of the creative efforts of many was a service in which the puppets on poles were carried down the center aisle amid the reading of scripture and the angelic voices of youth choir anthems and congregationally sung carols and, oh yes, little ones sitting quietly in amazement.

If we want to take children in worship seriously there are several ways this can happen:

- *Use their gifts:* Include prayers they have written, bulletin covers they have drawn, and hymns they have selected, and print the innocent but profound questions they have asked in the bulletin. These all help them to feel included.
- *Provide educational resources:* teach them and others the Christian story and its traditions. Tell a story about a hymn, include a bulletin insert that explains in age-appropriate language a scripture

lesson or liturgical tradition, or tell the scripture lesson as a children's drama. Include a bulletin insert about the scripture lesson for the service with questions for the family to discuss at the meal table.

- *Give a Children's Sermon or Meditation:* Good and effective children's sermons are frankly not easy to prepare and deliver. They can be as simple as a sensitive reading of a children's-book Bible story or as free-spirited as jumping on a pogo stick while shouting out "Christ is Risen!" The first challenge, again, is always to think like a child. The second is being able to relate to children on their level. To do this one must be agile and flexible in mind, body, and spirit. There will be shifts and turns in the road as childlike spontaneity takes over.

In a festival service the Sunday before Christmas, every seat was full and several hundred small children were ready to come forward for the children's sermon. I looked at my colleague, who I thought was the person to enthrall the little ones with the innocent message of Jesus. He looked at me and mouthed the words "I thought it was your turn." So much for collegial communication during the busy Advent season! I looked frantically for something to use for a Christmas object lesson. As the hymn was concluding and the children were coming forward, I noticed the Christmas tree covered with Christian symbols. I remembered a lesson about the candy cane I had used in a former parish. I knew there was a symbolic shepherd's staff on the tree that when turned upside down made a "J" for Jesus. One problem, the tree was covered with dozens of Chrismons (Christ monograms) and I couldn't find the shepherd's staff. The children sermon begins. "On our tree are symbols for Jesus. Let's see if we can find one that looks like a candy cane." We need to be able to be flexible and go off script.

The presentation of a children's sermon involves a number of considerations:

- *Make a decision regarding which age group is the primary focus.* A preschool child is obviously at a different faith development stage than a fourth grader. Older children can be involved by helping the younger children with their answers.

- *Try an audiovisual approach,* even a five-sense approach. Their senses are fully alive.
- *Be sensitive to the vocabulary that will be used.* While not stooping to baby talk, this is not a time to show that your vocabulary is extensive and multisyllabic.
- *Use body language that is open and welcoming.* Depending on the setting and seating arrangement for the children, either sitting or walking among them lets them know "this is for you, and you are special."
- *Involve them.* Be careful how you phrase your questions, and beware of children who try to dominate. Try to involve every child, even the shy ones.
- *Be brief, and limit points.* This is not the time to preach an adult sermon in miniature. It is a time for one theme for little ones, who often have short attention spans. A good children's sermon should take less than five minutes.
- *Occasionally include a reminder object that can be taken home,* such as a note with a scripture lesson, a prayer, a picture to color, an object that is a reminder of the point of the children's sermon, etc. Avoid sugary candy; their teachers and their parents will thank you.

When children are in worship, it is good to let the little ones and their spirit of innocence infuse that spirit in the big ones through effective worship planning.

And Then There Are the Emerging Big People

Far more complicated than the inclusion of children in worship is the ongoing challenge of making worship relevant and inspiring to the next generation of those who choose to be associated with a local church. Their decision regarding personal involvement in a faith community will be greatly influenced by what they experience in worship. It seems our postmodern era provides yet another new context that calls for worship to reform itself so that its flow, images, and spirit speak to another generation. The age in which we live is shaped by new forms of connectivity, like social networking, constantly changing technologies, the rapidity of mobility, and a constantly expanding worldview. A major response to these realities has been the emergent-church-and-worship movement. The nationally known pastor Rick Warren, in the foreword to the emergent-church leader Dan Kimball's book *The Emerging Church* wrote: "Never attach your church to a single style; it will become passé and outdated."[4] For some time now there has been an exodus from creedal, mainline historic churches. They have lost their ability to easily let go of old and lifeless rituals and traditions.

The challenge of the emergent-worship movement is nothing new. God has always called the church to be elastic and flexible and open to a new thing. Again let us remember that Jesus spoke of this when he used the image of old and new wineskins. Others of his parabolic references dealt with growth and change—"See the mustard seed." The church has constantly faced the test of how to pass along a two-thousand-year-old message so that it is heard and received by each new age. The evolution of worship to a new age can be a renewing, instead of a divisive, activity.

Because many churches are not large enough to offer multiple worship style opportunities, creative trial and error in the shaping of the liturgy is essential. There is even a benefit to having only one service. The one-body-many-parts call of the Gospel can be lived out in the creation of blended worship.

The response to the call from post-modern seekers has offered the blended worship concept. This form of worship has sought to merge the best of the past with the best of the new. It has sought to allow multiple generations worshipping together to learn an appreciation for the past and an openness to the new. It is a blessing to create blended worship opportunities that unite cross-generational worshippers. Being committed to creativity in blended worship, I personally have been fortunate to team with colleagues with expertise in the arts and technology. In implementing blended worship:

- Keep reminding the members that we are a diverse community and our worship needs to reflect that diversity.
- Keep current culturally through study and conversations with the emerging generation.
- Be certain that in the liturgy there is at least a little something for everyone. In its simplest manifestation, vary the hymns; use contemporary and historic.
- When introducing blended worship, do not make drastic changes to the order of worship. Vary the ways each section of the liturgy is presented.
- Start by brainstorming on what might be done with colleagues and members of the congregation.
- Seek common elements when transitioning to blended worship. For example, if transitioning into the use of jazz, start with familiar big band music, a music that bridges the generations. Why not have the choir sing "Unforgettable" as a metaphor for our love of God?
- Consider the worship practices of other Christian and even non-Christian traditions. Remember our global society; consider prayer practices particularly from Eastern religions. African and Native American practices, particularly the use of percussion, are being used more and more in many churches.
- Consider using technology that would give depth and excitement to the worship experience.
- Consider the use of art in all its forms: dance, film, contemporary theater, the visual arts, and the culinary arts. Even much secular art contains themes that speak of the human condition and the search for meaning and the Holy.

The truth is worship in the Christian church has always been emerging, trying to make the Gospel speak to every new generation. When questioned by some who wanted to hold worship captive to the past I'd remind them that Bach was a revolutionary in his musical era. And as clergy in a denomination that began with English separatists (Puritans and Pilgrims), I would remember that our ancestors called the organ "the devil's windbag" and that if we want to hold rigidly to our past, the organ and other musical instrumentation have to go.

Being the producer and the prompter in the theater of the Spirit are overwhelming roles to play. But the rewards are immeasurable as we watch seekers of God's presence experiencing the mystery and awe through some moment of encounter with God that is beyond articulation. The sense of fulfillment for us is deeply satisfying when worshippers experience a moment of divine serendipity with an "aha" of spiritual insight engaging their spirits. As those called to plan and lead worship we are blessed. Thanks be to God!

Inspiration

"As worship begins in holy expectancy, it ends in holy obedience. Holy obedience saves worship from becoming an opiate, an escape from the pressing needs of modern life." —Richard J. Foster[1]

Prayer

Holy One, fill us with your Holy Spirit as we produce and prompt in worship so the worship space will be filled with the awes and ahas that testify to our connecting ourselves with You. We know that you are watching our performance, so we will try to act in ways that glorify Your name. Amen.

9

Faith Development

Seize the Moment

Body Building Exercises

- Who played a significant role in your faith development?
- What settings most profoundly affected that development?
- Take a moment to visualize those people whose role was significant and identify the gifts that made them effective teachers of faith. Offer a prayer of thanksgiving for their ministry.

Recently there has been no end to surveys that announce the ignorance of a significant majority of Christians when it comes to their Bible literacy. Gallup, Pew, and other respected research organizations have confirmed the illiteracy of an alarmingly large portion of the Christian community. In a Gallup poll, only four of ten self-acknowledged Christians knew the Sermon on the Mount was given by Jesus. In a Barna survey, only 9 percent of Christians knew what the Great Commission was. Only 25 percent of "born again" Christians knew that in that commissioning Jesus was compelling us "to go to all the world and teach what I have commanded you." Such statistics make us laugh; otherwise we would cry.[1] Boston University professor Stephen Prothero was so acutely aware of religious illiteracy that in 2007 he wrote a book, *Religious Literacy: What Every American Needs to Know—And Doesn't.* It was a best seller.[2]

Early in my ministry I was asked by the chair of the board of deacons where I served if I would arrange for the confirmation class questioning by board members. He also asked that I supply them with the questions. While I was leery of this form of "testing," I was young and acquiesced. On the evening of the "inquisition," during the first round of questions, I watched in disbelief as many wrong answers were accepted by the board members. Once the young people had gone home, I was surrounded by some of the church "leaders" and reprimanded for not including the answers. These were the most basic of Bible and faith questions. Here was one more profound testimony to the failure of the church to provide a sound and life-changing program of faith and spiritual development.

Faith development is more than the acquisition of rote knowledge. It is more expansive than merely memorizing scripture verses or retelling of faith history stories. Faith development also includes the imbedding of the deeper meaning of those verses and stories into the personal spiritual life and daily activities of each Christian. Faith development should foster a personal relationship with God and the public practice of their Christian values.

There are numerous well-documented reasons for this faith ignorance. A June 2009 *Wall Street Journal* article on the decline of the church school, one historic mainstay in passing along foundations of our faith, is well known. "A number of reasons can be given for the decline, including an increasingly secular society and the other demands on the time of the average child. And then there is a content problem. The kind of Sunday school activities that pleased my generation simply wouldn't fly with today's busier and more sophisticated kids. A lot of the stuff we did was rote memory," said a leading Baptist educator.[3] Also, mobility and new family patterns, including youth sports, make faithful church attendance problematic. While many of the traditional models for the delivery of the faith can be continued, there must be new, creative, dynamic ways to nurture and enhance our ministry of Christian faith development. While the church school and other scheduled educational offerings may be helpful ways of nurturing faith development, a more expansive vision of numerous other delivery systems needs to be considered.

This broader vision will require us to think creatively about what professional educators call "educable moments." By this they mean there are moments when there is a heightened receptivity for learning. For example:

- A student's wallet is stolen. This provides no better time to reflect on victimization, potential reasons for theft, and consequences of stealing. In a biblical context this would be a time to study in depth the Eighth Commandment.
- An incident of racial or religious bigotry is front-page news. What better time to set aside the planned curriculum and immediately design a cross-racial or interfaith dialogue with others in the community?
- A hands-on mission project of rehabbing homes in the lower income areas in a nearby city takes place. What better time to discuss the issues of poverty and the biblical texts that address the poor than within a few days of the outreach?
- You are drawn to a work of art at your office that you never noticed before. What an opportunity for a personal devotional moment or to discuss with a colleague his or her thoughts on the work.

Educable moments will appear unexpectedly, and the church leader needs to respond quickly. Such moments are fleeting.

Every moment has the potential to be a teachable one. One of the mottos of my life comes from the poet Theodore Roethke: "I learn by going where I have to go."[4] Every moment is a moment that can bring faith insights. God is subtle and has placed a potential for learning divine wisdom into every here and now. It is incumbent on the church leader to be aware of this reality and design faith development programs that operate both inside and outside of traditional church education settings.

We must expand the classroom. Every place becomes a faith learning space. The planning process for total awareness in educable-moment teaching begins with reflection of our daily lives and where we find ourselves. (See Appendix C, Educable Moment Exercise.) Once the day's doings have been dissected, then creative teaching will emerge. For those in a business setting, a devotional resource could be developed such as one-minute readings or prayers before meetings. During sermon preparation, a text, phone call, or e-mail to parishioners about their understanding of the text could become a faith development opportunity. Gardeners could be asked to write journal entries or brief prayers based on their seasonal experiences. These could be included in a church devotion booklet or online resource. Podcasts and recorded sermons make drive time an educational moment. In several of my parishes it became apparent that family meal time was a together time that could be used for church talk. A weekly bible reflection was designed for cross-generational mealtime discussion. Mealtime graces written by church-school children and adults were also included. The response to these mealtime moments was overwhelmingly positive. The creative leader must be vigilant about seeing each moment as a teachable one.

In the local church setting itself we are often minimalist and uncreative in our ways of teaching and reflecting on the Good News. We have limited our understanding of faith development to formal classes, seminars, workshops, etc. Within the setting of the church building and its surrounding campus, subtle educational stimuli can lead to meaningful faith and spiritual development. A strong emphasis needs to be placed on making all church space education space. From developing an outdoor environmental study program on a larger campus to displaying church artists' paintings and photography in a mini-gallery, nothing is impossible. For these gallery displays, both professionals and amateurs, including church-school children, could be encouraged to write a simple faith statement or prayer to accompany their artwork. Whether the art is secular or sacred, the spiritual themes are in abundance as catalysts for the inspiration for a work of art. Consider "Living Water," for example, works could include such visual elements as lakes, oceans, raindrops, puddles, and drinking glasses. We need to adopt a perspective that every square foot of space can provide an opportunity for spiritual growth. Faith-development opportunities surround us if we only look and consider the possibilities.

People were at first puzzled at the signs throughout the church building and property that read, "Warning!" "Pay Attention!" "God is Here!" "Stop, Look, and Listen!" The ancient sycamore tree in the parsonage front yard; the cluttered fellowship hall kitchen; the narthex of the sanctuary; the doorway leading to the education-wing classrooms; the walls over the water fountain in the entrance hallway to the church offices and over the copier—all announced the same "Pay attention" message. Since it is well documented that to pay attention is the key that opens the door to an encounter with the Holy, the essence of faith formation, we need to be fervent in our attempts to use our space to call seekers to attention. As Evelyn Underhill wrote, "For lack of attention a thousand forms of loveliness elude us every day."[5]

Along with its opportunities for praise, community building, proclamation, and rededication, worship is a prime-time opportunity for teaching. It is sad to admit, but the worship hour and the following fellowship time are often the only hours when most Christians will be physically present in the church building. So there's another challenge. How does one expand the homily and liturgy to add an educational dimension for this captive audience? How should the worship program be formatted, and what should it include? How should the sanctuary space be best used? Why not use the worship bulletin as an educational and liturgical resource? Historical comments and devotional notes could be included with a selected hymn. Original weekly inserts (or directions to the pastor's blog) on the scripture theme would offer faith-development opportunities. On occasion the architecture of the church could be highlighted and symbols or stained glass interpreted. Sometimes a reflective question can be posed before the Gospel. The aim of weaving education as intentional faith formation into the worship has as its ultimate goal stimulation for further discussion outside the church context. Faith images and words that are left unexplained can be a source of discussion on the ride home. It's all about continuing the education.

A key to the success of any attempts at immersion education is the creation of thought-provoking questions. While most church communication is intended to notify, it can also aim to raise introspective questions. Bulletins and inserts can prompt spiritual journeys: "What does this artwork say about the call to care and your dedication to justice?" "How does this Scripture passage make you feel as you think about your work relationships?" "Where do the words or melody of this hymn lead you?" One might try asking open-ended questions to be answered in the following weeks. Or the questions could lead to a type of scavenger hunt for symbols within the church architectural or worship space. Whether it is a take-home resource of questions for after a fellowship gathering at a play or movie presentation, or an outline of conversation starters that follows a renewal of marriage vows, these are all catalysts for spiritual growth. Jesus, in good rabbinic teaching style, frequently issued calls for his followers to pay attention and listen for the answers to life's most important questions.

Taking advantage of educational moments and provocative questions are but two ways that can empower faith development. Intergenerational education is frequently neglected as a primary teaching resource. Too often there is segregation by age, marital status, or sex. Dr. Holly Allen, a Lutheran educator, has done extensive research into the benefits of intergenerational education. She discovered that before the Common Era, Judaism primarily used intergenerationally based education. This was also the model in early Christianity. While we need to acknowledge that some education has to be based on age-appropriate instruction, a well-designed intergenerational program brings a deeper understanding to our faith than segregated instruction might offer. Allen affirms the richness of intergenerational faith development: "Intergenerational Christian faith development groups are authentic complex learning environments, made up of individuals at various stages in their Christian journey, teaching some, learning from others, as they participate in their community of believers."[6]

The church is one of the few places where the generations meet. There is a depth of faith development that can happen when the segregation by age or other criteria is eliminated. A greater dedication is needed to find opportunities to foster intergenerational teaching and learning experiences. Designing these opportunities does take considerable effort. Activities must be included that are meaningful to the diverse developmental stages, that allow for a respect for both the innocent wisdom of children and the life-honed wisdom of the aged. The fruits of well-designed efforts are manifold. During a bimonthly after-church intergenerational luncheon Bible study, I was profoundly moved to observe seasoned citizens attentively listening as a first grader explained the meaning of a colored marker drawing based on a selected parable of Jesus. I have been amazed at how those same seasoned citizens tried to choose words that would allow even younger children to understand some profound time-tested insights about their faith. In that same setting, I have been amused and brought to divine laughter as learners of all ages danced together singing "Bananas for the Lord." With their arms waving and feet circling, all interpreted Jesus' words "I am the vine and you are the branches." I have been brought to the edge of tears as small children from a Sunday school class visited with an aging homebound member and asked him about his favorite Bible stories.

One of the most fertile fields for intergenerational education is the confirmation program. Many churches see it as process of leave-taking from parents as youth arrive at their age of discernment concerning their faith. In some churches the confirmation program begins with a ritualized leave-taking ceremony. With such a sharp point of separation, opportunities for a true passing on of the faith traditions from generation to generation is lost. A well-designed multigenerational program that includes the adolescent confirmand, parents, and faith mentors can enrich the faith development of all of the participants. A multifaceted program where confirmands meet together but with opportunities also for meeting with parents or church-member sponsors models the way that the faith has been handed down throughout history. Each class may vary in approach from intergenerational small group discussions to shared art activities to educational gaming techniques to travel opportunities. Imagine intergenerational opportunities in which the participants:

- Are asked to create in clay their image of God and explain it.
- Discuss a faith-based response to issues such as stealing, same-sex marriage, poverty, tithing, sexual mores.
- Serve in a soup kitchen together and discuss their impressions of the experience as people of faith.
- View a film or popular TV show together and reflect on the values expressed in the film or show.
- Answer together some challenging questions about a passage in the Bible.

- Share a meal with an adult sponsor as the sponsor shares her or his faith journey.
- Visit convalescing members of the church and listen to their faith stories.
- Write together a devotional resource that includes lessons from life wisdom, scripture, secular thinkers, and personal thoughts.

The unmistakable goal is the education of all participants and the passing of the wisdom and rituals of the faith from generation to generation. The success of such programming will be evident in the long-term relationships between the students and their faith mentors. There will be a new respect between the youth and their parents as they learn models for communication based on an openness and trust that can be used in other familial settings.

There is no question that mainline denominations and congregations need to look for and develop new models of intergenerational education. This is particularly essential since a majority of churches in many denominations have fewer than two-hundred-member churches.

The declining faith-development ministry of the local church requires energetic leadership emboldened to go beyond the traditional models of education and the limited worship time boundaries. Effective pastors or lay leaders need to grasp an educable-moment theory that expands the classroom. They need to see every place as a learning space and need to select or create more programs that use an intergenerational model of learning. It will not be effortless. Yet with the new societal realities, if this is not attempted, religious illiteracy will increase. (See Appendix D, Getting Started in Inclusive Youth Ministry.)

Inspiration

"Jesus taught that whenever we discover truth, it is God who has taught us. No book is so bad that you can't get some truth out of it. No person is without some truth to teach us. No situation is without its truth. God is instructing us in the soul sciences and soul arts every second of every day."

—Leonard Sweet[7]

Prayer

Ever revealing, never concealing God, keep surprising us with new revelations of your grace and love wherever we may be. Lead us through the moments and events of each day to ask the life-enhancing and faith-affirming questions that we need to ponder. Give us the trust to go out in faith not knowing, but knowing that you will give us the faith and divine wisdom to know where we need to go. In the name of the Incarnate Teacher, we pray this. Amen.

10

The Smell of Coffee and the Shack in the Room

A Church Immersed in Wider Mission

Body Building Exercises

- When people enter your church, how would they know it's committed to going out to all the world in mission?
- As a pastor or church leader, what is your role in the ministry of wider mission?
- Define the roles of a mission or outreach committee.

The aroma of coffee pervaded the large fellowship hall. Voices were competing for attention. A few church leaders were discussing with other leaders some of the issues that arose at their last committee meeting. Children were getting a sugar high eating some of the donuts and pastries on the fellowship-hour table. None of the fruits and vegetables offered appealed to their tastes. And in the midst of it all there was a pile of variously shaped plywood, bags of cement, and corrugated plastic. Members of the youth fellowship stood guard around this odd intrusion of what appeared to be junk and building supplies. As curiosity rose, one person at a time would ask, "What's this all about?" Again and again the answer was repeated: "These are the building supplies for a fifteen-by-fifteen-foot home in the poorest barrio of Guatemala City." Then the young person handed the questioner a sheet which included facts about world poverty. Along with coffee, an appetite for wider mission was also being brewed.

> "The Spirit of the Lord is upon me, because he has anointed me to bring good news to the poor. He has sent me to proclaim

> release to the captives and recovery of sight to the blind, to let the oppressed go free." (Lk 4:18)
>
> "And Jesus came and said to them, 'All authority in heaven and on earth has been given to me. Go therefore and make disciples of all nations, baptizing them in the name of the Father and of the Son and of the Holy Spirit, and teaching them to obey everything that I have commanded you. And remember, I am with you always, to the end of the age.' " (Mt 28:18–20)

Christ's words are validating enough to make it clear that the ultimate ministry of the local church is to go to all the world in service to the sick, the poor, the excluded. There is also the underlying theme of advocating for the rights of the voiceless, the marginalized in our world, all those who do not have the physical or personal power to plead their own cases. In the local church, two wings are needed to allow it to soar in its ministry, the wing of inreach and the wing of outreach. Inreaching ministries strengthen the personal spiritual life of the members so they feel emboldened to participate in the essential ministry of the church: outreach. It was the eighteenth- and nineteenth-century Baptist missionary to India William Carey who best summed up this concept of the two wings of ministry: "To know the will of God, we need an open Bible and an open map."[1] All of our ministries should be aimed at helping those who desire to follow Christ in moving beyond selfish concerns through selfless service to others. The ultimate goal of our efforts is to play our small part in building the realm of God, shaping a world where shalom, the peace that passes all understanding, is experienced by all.

If we take seriously the call of Christ to go, and accept the challenges that going entails, the church must foster a total immersion concept of wider mission. From the entranceway of the church to its programs and worship content, there ought to be an obvious display of selfless service as the centerpiece of the Gospel we proclaim. All members and visitors should immediately know they are immersed in mission. The immersion experience should tell stories, give information, raise questions, and lead people to personal outreach opportunities.

Immersion Begins Immediately

A new arrival in town comes to the church office of the Old First Church to meet the pastor, who is currently in the midst of a counseling session which should conclude in fifteen minutes. The secretary offers the person a cup of Fair Trade coffee and leads her to a chair in the church library. On the walls is the monthly art show. Church and local artists, as well as children in the church school, have drawn, photographed, or painted art with a common theme: peacemaking. On several of the tables there are clay sculptures done by in-need young people from a local pottery learning center. The newcomer picks up the church newsletter and learns of two very intriguing mission projects. The first article is a quarterly letter from a missionary in Ghana whom the church supports. The other is even more fascinating. It seems that the previous month's newsletter posed a question: Where should a Christian stand on the issue of gun control? Short answers to the question were solicited and published anonymously in the newsletter, others could be viewed on a bulletin board in the social hall.

(To be continued)

If the church is called to empower its members to go to all the world, both near and far, then one important role of the church is to be a center for diversity education and global awareness. It is called to break open provincial understandings and narrow worldviews that are still pervasive in common culture. It is to make the concept of the welfare of the larger community, not individual self-centeredness, the defining factor in how we live our lives. The writer Rick Marinis offers a keen and, for some, hard-to-swallow reality about life: "Kings and cabbages go back to the compost, but good deeds stay green forever. . . . Under the skin we are all related . . . members of the same humble club, say what you will about superficial differences."[2] The church is to open the minds and hearts of its members in both word and deed to the oneness that Christ sought to teach his disciples. It is this oneness that the

Good Samaritan parable and the story of the woman at Jacob's Well illustrate differences are trumped by the truth that we all share the same human journey.

Another concept the church should cultivate in its wider mission efforts is the important difference between a hand up and a handout. While often overused, "Give me a fish and I will eat for a day, teach me to fish and I will eat for a lifetime" is a foundational guiding principle for mission work. Along with feeding the starving we must offer them the educational and developmental resources to feed themselves. We must provide them with the power to have a stake in shaping their own destiny. While a soup kitchen ministry is important, probably equally or more important are the ministries of education and job training for those who are the guests at the meals served there. Jesus gave a hand up so that those held back, whether by illness or prejudice, could be self-sufficient and become contributors to the community. The ministry of empowerment, though, does not offer the instant feedback that charitable gifts may bring. The ministry of empowerment can be disquieting. When power is shared, those who have been helped may suddenly want to have an equal voice in creating their future. There is a difference between ministries of bent-knee charity and ministries that seek to share power so that the in-need person or community plays a partnership role in overcoming the need. It is an eye-to-eye relationship.

There were sixty-four children and sixty-four mentors as partners in an "I Have a Dream" program. The program promised its in-need participants a scholarship for higher education if the students graduated from high school. It was the hope that committed mentors would help the participants reach this goal. The graduation rate for high risk students in Hartford, Connecticut, was under 50 percent. While the mentors were very successful in their ministry during the six-year period, they had to make special efforts to involve parents in the decision-making process about their child's education. The power sharing was not always easy when cultural and socioeconomic factors intervened. But without that power sharing, the program would have been a failure. Ours is a ministry of equal-to-equal empowerment not bent-knee charity.

(The immersion continues)

> The pastor comes into the library and invites the newcomer into her office. On the coffee table is a Bible and the denominational mission calendar of prayer. At the end of their conversation the pastor gives the visitor a brochure about the church in which, along with the worship, musical, social, and educational life of the church, is a section on the church's mission and outreach programs. The brochure contains the same information as the church website. On the website there is a registration form for monthly soup kitchen service opportunities. There's also a list of the church's bimonthly and summer travel mission immersion programs. The list is lengthy: local Habitat for Humanity building projects, a trip to Washington to learn from the denomination's Washington justice group, Habitat for Humanity winter trip to Honduras, and summer mission trips to urban social service programs and a Native American reservation. During a church tour the newcomer sees an ESL (English as a second language) class in progress, a senior-citizens advocacy group office, an upscale thrift shop whose $60,000 annual proceeds fund mission programs, and the church's preschool program. In the small chapel, the talented youth choir is rehearsing for a trip to Boston, where they will sing at a benefit for an inner-city social service organization. The newcomer tells the pastor that she and her husband and children will be at worship the next Sunday morning.

What are the foundations on which a wider mission church is built? There are at least four catalysts in building such a church:

- an openness to the challenging Word of the Bible
- a pastor who is committed to hands-on mission experiences
- a readiness to empower the impassioned
- an outreach or mission committee that is not a banking institution

There was an awkward moment during one partner-church Bible study when a usually reticent African American woman made a statement that made almost everyone else in her group feel uncomfortable. Her downtown city church counterparts seemed a little uneasy thinking that her words might have offended their guests. The all-white suburban church guests were at a loss for words. The study was on the Beatitudes. "Yes, in Matthew it says poor in spirit. But turn to Luke 6:20. It says blessed are the poor . . . period. This is about Jesus really being concerned about poor folks. I consider you my friends, but this passage isn't about you." Once the shock wore off, a healthy discussion about Matthew's concern for a humble spirit and Luke's concern for the poor and outcast followed. While Jesus does focus much of his preaching and teaching on spiritual and character change, he does press strongly for alleviating the plight of the poor and outcast. The reality is that both the Hebrew and Christian scriptures, when addressing personal shalom or well-being (salvation), tie such salvation to the welfare and salvation of the wider community. I remember well the words of a faithful attendee of a weekly Bible study: "It seems that Jesus spends a lot of time with hurting people and Paul is constantly calling for people of different backgrounds to get together." The church that has a mission heart studies the Word for its comfort as well as its challenge to go and serve.

In another case, some seminary seniors were dismayed at news they heard about their upcoming seminar abroad. All of the previous classes had traveled to Germany and toured the great historic venues of Western European Christendom and in the evening lounged in the beer halls discussing the likes of theological giants like Barth, Brunner, and Bonhoeffer. The dreams of German beer halls and majestic cathedrals with spires vaulting to the heavens had been replaced by nightmares of mosquitoes, Montezuma's revenge, and uncomfortable bus rides on poorly paved or unpaved roads in Jamaica or Honduras and other impoverished Caribbean and Central American countries. Good German beer was usurped by rice and frijoles. Yet that seminar abroad shaped the hearts of it journeyers, I being mong them, more than any lecture on the great theologians of Western Europe. We all returned on fire and with hearts committed to wider mission. There are so many hands-on mission experiences available in our world of global travel today that it is almost impossible not to have had a firsthand experience of getting close to the realities of poverty. Pastors and leaders of wider mission-committed churches need to regularly avail themselves of national and international service opportunities and encourage their members to join them on their journeys of compassionate service. Such hands-on service with the poor and marginalized puts a face on poverty and brings the participants into contact with people who teach the meaning of faith in the midst of their daily adversity.

(The immersion continues . . .)

As the newcomer and her family enter the sanctuary they are given a worship bulletin and a children's bulletin. Once they take their seats they begin to scan the children's bulletin and a bulletin insert which includes a reproduction of a pen-and-ink drawing by the Dutch artist Albrecht Dürer. It is of a homeless family in the streets of a major city. A question appears on the bulletin: "What does it feel like to be without a home?" A prayer for the homeless in the world follows this question. The children's bulletin has a picture of Jesus surrounded by children of diverse racial and cultural backgrounds. The back of the bulletin has a form to fill out and place in the offering plate or drop off or mail to the church office. It is an information-gathering form in preparation for a future discipleship Sunday. The form asks the person to list the volunteer social service organizations in which he or she is involved. The church's involvement goal is clearly stated with these challenging words: "Whether through the church or through other organizations, we're aiming for 100 percent involvement in some form of wider mission." As the newcomers read the calendar they note that three Alcoholics Anonymous meetings are held in the church every week. There are also a cancer support group, a widow and widower group, and a divorce support group that use the building weekly. Counting the outreach groups she noticed during her tour of the building, the

> woman saw a total of twelve outreach ministries, including a new Hispanic church, which uses the church's chapel and several classrooms for its burgeoning ministry. At the time of the announcements a member of the youth group speaks from the lectern inviting all members of the church to join them on their annual "Hartford by Night" tour. The church vans will leave at 6:00 p.m. and return at 1:00 a.m. Rather than enjoying a gourmet dinner and show, the group will serve meals at a shelter for battered women and their children. This will be followed by visits to the hospital emergency room and morgue, a meeting with members of the police department, and a visit to a suicide-prevention answering service. A late-evening snack will be sought at an all-night diner.

Within every community of faith, there are people who have a passion for bringing good news to the poor and doing their small part to usher in the realm of God right here and right now. They are an important asset in giving enthusiasm to a church's outreach ministries. They are often involved in programs outside the church context that are for the betterment of their community and world. They might be involved in a local group seeking to address the issue of world hunger or have a commitment to educational programs for Native American children. Their energy and passion for outreach is a resource on which a vital wider mission ministry can be focused. While understanding that they should not promote their particular cause at the expense of all others, they can become educators in the field of their outreach interest. Their interests can become some of the spokes in the wheel of the church's mission involvements. By inviting them to take on leadership responsibilities, it should be made clear that there are no promises of mission-dollars being allotted to the organization that they support.

A key component in a dynamic outreach ministry is having a committee of zealous mission souls who do not see themselves as a mission dollars' banking institution. The question to ask outreach and mission committees is "What would your committee do if you had no money to distribute in the name of the church?" The reality is that a significant portion of these committees spend inordinate amounts of time and energy making decisions about the distribution of money (often a small amount) to the requests of dozens of good causes. The stories of committees spending enormous amounts of time on whether the church should send $300 or $375 to a particular worthy cause has led many creative and activist souls to avoid participation. We must go beyond and set aside this banking institution concept if the church is to be immersed in mission. There are important functions that those responsible for the in wider mission of the church should carry out. Such committees should do the following:

- *Educate:* Whether it be building shacks in the midst of coffee hour, educational programs in the intergenerational study curriculum, inserts with pithy questions in the bulletin, pictures of mission on the church's video monitor in the hallway, hunger simulation games, creative dramatic teasers in the worship service, being educators is the most important role of those inspired individuals who oversee the wider mission ministry of the church.
- *Advocate:* An important part of any outreach committee's function is to advocate for causes that help create a more just society. Occasionally taking a well-researched stand for justice, even if it might be controversial for a few in the congregation, is best handled by the laity as a way of deflecting tensions away from the pastor. To minimize controversy in the advocacy ministry, often raising the question "What is right and Christian in addressing this difficult issue?" creates a less divisive spirit within the congregation. The more the entire congregation participates in shaping the church's justice positions, the greater impact the action will have. The final stance is often less important than the discussion that precedes it. The themes of diversity and an expanded worldview should permeate this advocacy ministry.
- *Separate:* There are so many calls from worthy community, national, and global welfare organizations for the church's personal and financial resources. The committee can serve a vital role in assessing the impact of those organizations, their goals in light of the church's goal in wider mission, their potential for deeper involvement by church members, and their use of the resources

they receive from donors. Information from the organization, charitable-giving evaluative websites, and personal knowledge should be taken into consideration in the prioritizing process. This research can also provide information for individual church members' decisions on the use of their time, talent, and treasure. With limited resources, rational culling and prioritizing is necessary if the church is to use those resources most effectively.

- *Associate:* "Two are better than one, because they have a good reward for their toil." These words from chapter four of Ecclesiastes remind us that working with others, particularly in areas of meeting need, can bring large dividends in accomplishing mission. A crucial responsibility of an outreach or mission committee must be to seek partnerships with other organizations in tackling its goals. This is particularly important in smaller churches. Building alliances with other churches, social service organizations, community-service entities such as schools, fire departments, the department of social services, and community-betterment groups can bring good reward for the church's toil.

For those churches in a denominational structure, a significant partner in the wider mission effort is the judicatory of the national church. It can be particularly effective in addressing the global issues of poverty and injustice. For churches with limited resources, this link can be significant. Such an alliance can offer:

- a challenge to think globally when individuals want to think locally
- first-hand connections with missionaries serving throughout the world
- a commitment to the empowerment of the native population in addressing and solving poverty and injustice issues in their particular community
- hands-on mission opportunities
- resources that educate and personalize global issues

- more effective mission for the dollar because of alliances they have built with other religious denominations and associations, secular relief organizations, and health and welfare programs overseen by the native populations of the countries served
- a clearinghouse in determining the effectiveness of the numerous social service and wider mission organizations
- quick response aid to national and global tragedies

The building of alliances strengthens our outreach. So the first question that should be asked when seeking to respond to human need is "Are there others with whom we can join our efforts?"

- *Coordinate:* In many churches, various engagements are being made with wider mission ministries. For instance, the church school is raising money for a special hunger project; the men's and women's groups are supporting a missionary in Africa; the youth group is having a car wash for a refugee organization; the youth choir is having a fundraiser for their choir tour to Canada; the executive committee is urging members to support the One Great Hour of Sharing national church offering; the church's preschool is selling baked goods for a homeless shelter in the city; the church-sponsored Girl Scout troop is selling cookies at the coffee hour; a member of the mission committee has a passion for third-world small business and is selling woven goods from Central America; and so on. A helpful service an outreach or mission committee can perform is to coordinate groups by having the oversight of a common calendar, particularly of fundraisers. This coordinating role helps avoid a dilution of personal energies and financial stewardship because of overlap.

There will be financial resources to be divided and given to others who are seeking to build the realm of God here and now. However, the investment-banking portion of an outreach or mission committee should be well controlled so that it does not overshadow the rest of the committee's work. The recurring question of wider mission committees should be "What would we do if we had no money to work with or distribute?"

(The immersion continues . . .)

During the service, the prayer concerns are limited but still filled with requests for global-concern intercessions. The middle hymn is sung to a Chinese melody, and the Communion breads are a variety from different ethnic and cultural backgrounds. During the coffee hour, SERRV, an international economic development group, has products for sale made by overseas cottage industries. SERRV has a sale every other month. A whiteboard showing excerpts from the Saturday children's program in which five churches—African American, Hispanic, Lebanese Orthodox and two predominately Caucasian—had come together under the theme of "Let's All Get into the Boat Together." After being warmly greeted by church members, the newcomer and her family know, even though the pastor said nothing directly about wider mission in her sermon, that they were attending a church that was centered in Christ's call to go to all the world.

(Let the story of immersion begin in the church you lead)

Old First is a church immersed in mission. Many churches believe their members should be committed to mission outreach and think creatively about how every aspect of their ministries can be filled with missionary zeal. Not all churches can be as expansive in their immersion as Old First, but in churches of every size and setting, visitors who enter feel bathed in a spirit bringing the Good News of justice and righteousness to the marginalized, outcast, and very needy.

It is sometimes easy to smell the coffee and the shack. It is the role of the leadership of a local church to call its members' attention to the shack and the call of the Gospel to bring a foretaste of the realm of God to the least and the left out. Christ's disciples are called to go to all the world, not stay in comfortable, little cocoons created by the false god which proclaims, "Me first, we second."

Inspiration

Social justice has to do more with changing systems which, although often managed by people with good conscience, are evil in that they, knowingly or unknowingly, victimize certain people. Watch out for those sins of omission! —Ronald Rolheiser[3]

Prayer

God of justice, God of love, I am sometimes timid in raising the tough questions about justice that you call me to ask. God of righteousness, God of graciousness, the needs of the world seem so unsolvable that I would prefer to stick with the comfort, not the challenge, of the Gospel. When feeling I am overwhelmed or timid, remind me of the fulfillment of a victory for injustice won or guide me to a place where the face of poverty or need glares before my eyes. I pray all this in the name of the One who challenges those with a myopic worldview to expand their vision. Amen.

11

A Colonial Encounter with Twenty-First-Century Horsepower

Traditional and Nontraditional Church Growth Strategies and the Volkswagen Bug

Body Building Exercises

- What is your church's rationale for growth?
- Why would one want to become a member of your church?
- In one sentence, what would you like nonmembers to say about your church?

We want to examine ways to make our churches alluring to those who might want to visit and subsequently become involved in our life and ministry. Before going further we need to state unequivocally that church health is the foundational component that leads to church growth and successful evangelism. Keeping our eye on the target of church health is essential to keeping seekers coming back once they have come in.

But still there are strategies needed to lure strangers indoors for the first time. Let's put that sanctified word "evangelism" on hold as well. While it may sound grand and awe inspiring—proclaiming the Good News—most of those people who sit in the pews and provide committed lay leadership are focusing on the issue of church growth in less grandiose terms. Their reasons for evangelism are varied: bringing people to Jesus, finding more volunteers to help with church programs, letting others in on the joy and fulfillment of being together and serving together, increasing the budget by getting more money from more members. And let us also be honest about what evangelism really is:

marketing and advertising! We believe we have a good product and we want to sell it to others so they might benefit as we have. Peter's bold proclamations in the midst of large longing-for-something-better crowds could be considered a first-century infomercial. He was a satisfied buyer who wanted others to experience the feeling of well-being he received from buying—with his heart and soul—the product that Jesus sold. We have a product, participation in the body of Christ, that can bring peace of mind and peace to the world. Isn't that enough impetus to put together a comprehensive marketing strategy?

Sales and Marketing Strategies

One of the first components of church marketing is identifying our target audience. Whom do you want to attract? The answer to that question might be broad: all people seeking fulfillment and joy beyond their understanding. There should, though, be a primary target audience that is more defined. Many of the fastest-growing churches have selected their audiences and then shaped their programs around the desires and wants of a particular demographic. A church in a community that is and will be for retired folks, while wanting to have an intergenerational membership, will design its program largely for a mature (in age) congregation. In a fast-growing suburb, populated by young families, the church's programs will reflect a desire to attract young people. If the church interprets the Bible literally, those who hold to a metaphorical interpretation will not be the prime audience for marketing strategies. Even when the goal is to be a church that seeks unity in Christ through diversity, the way the church's ministries are shaped is defined by that more expansive demographic audience.

Whether through the process of writing a mission statement or through a simple survey asking members to complete the sentence: "We are the church that ________________________________." Defining the church's descriptive phrase is the key element in church growth. We are a church that puts wider mission first, or we are a church that focuses on eclectic worship, or we are a church that desires to be inclusive. Having a well-defined understanding of the particular style and mission of your church will give focus to shaping the church's ministry decisions and will set your church apart from others selling a similar product.

A second key marketing strategy is not to start advertising the product until it has been tested and attractively packaged. We need to take the time and effort to get our house in order for visitors. When new visitors are coming to our homes, we mow the lawn, put the dirty laundry away, straighten the slanting pictures, and put out the best dinnerware or party decorations. Too often churches are impatient about church growth and invite guests before everything is in order. We need to remember that we may very well have only one chance to sell our product.

It is useful to look at the church, inside and outside, as a stranger would. If the property is not well maintained or is stark and cold, landscaping might be needed. If primary entranceways are unappealing and looking worn, refurbishing or even remodeling may be required. Depending on the target audience, details of the main inside and outside areas need to be evaluated. From the selection of plants and flowers to the color of the walls, from the cleanliness of playground areas to the selection of artwork in the halls, from decisions on the comfort of the pews to the technology (or lack thereof) used to welcome and quickly acquaint the visitor with the church and its mission, the little details must be considered and addressed before an intensive, long-term marketing effort is begun. Even in the oldest of church buildings with a minimal budget, renewal can take place.

Often overlooked attraction tools are the church sign and the use of banners and other outdoor media. The basic facts need to be clearly displayed on the primary church sign: the church's name, times of services, church phone number. Depending on the size of the sign, the title of next Sunday's sermon is a helpful addition to the basic information. Listing the names of the clergy may just waste space. In some cases town zoning will limit the possibility of a sign whose size can hold this information and which can be seen from a distance. Occasional canvas and vinyl signs announcing a special event can help attract nonmembers. Even some of the most sedate and awesome church structures can have an image change with well-designed and strategically placed banners. Imagine a lengthy banner hanging from a majestic steeple announcing in vibrant sunrise colors, "Christ is Risen." Consider flames of the Spirit on a Pentecost Sunday blowing in the wind from a flagpole. How about a banner created from children's art draped across the entrance to the church on a special children's recognition Sunday?

Signage can play a huge role when it comes to changing the appearance and image of a church. For large, meandering older buildings, signage and directional aids are essential. We are offering a way into the Gospel so the lost may be found. Let us make sure that those who have found us do not get lost. Clear signage and then a human encounter with someone who can welcome and direct is essential. Recently a modestly sized church held an expansion project, hoping to gain more visibility in the community. The offices were placed on the third floor of the new structure. A lavish entranceway with a video monitor greeted the visitor. Even with the new sleek tech splash, something was amiss. Soon a small desk was purchased and added to the entrance. So the twenty-million-dollar campaign had overlooked the most welcoming technique of all, a real live person. A church building without a smile and a handshake is incomplete. Along with meeting physical accessibility issues, having resources that provide a roadmap for the stranger to the church building is essential. We desire that all can gain access to our buildings and so must be vigilant that no one is lost.

Developing the Product

Equally important to advertising and marketing is delivering. The customers had better find the programs we're selling when they come through our doors. While churches will always maintain at least some broad spectrum of ministry opportunities for all, the programs in some overt way need to be in sync with who we say we are or aspire to be. If we are the church of eclectic worship, we had better have worship services that surprise and are varied. If we tell the world we're a church that puts mission first, this had better be our focus. If strangers visit as the product is being developed we can say, "Stick with us, we are working on it." Most consumers are looking for the finished or always new and improving product. In large-membership churches the particular staff talents are also a reflection of the vision. If the church is not ready to receive new customers, the potential for future membership growth is actually damaged by negative publicity it receives from those who came to the church to sample the product that was advertised. It pays to take the time to be ready in all aspects of a church's life and ministry.

Training the Sales Reps

We also need to prepare the sales representatives for their roles. Survey after survey of people who have joined churches identify the primary reason for first coming to the church as having been invited by a member. Members are the field sales representatives for any local church, yet many are ill prepared for their role. Often there is an acute discomfort in getting to "the ask." Opportunities for potential new-member growth are stifled by laity who keep silent about their religious life and the church they attend. Sometimes there's unease about faith talk; it's a private matter. "I'm afraid people might think I'm one of those religious fanatics if I start talking about faith and my church," was the response of one church member when asked why she didn't invite her neighbors to worship. A simple but effective response to the uneasiness of the laity to be evangelists for their local church is an occasional training resource for the church's field sales representatives. Such things as an article in the church newsletter, an insert in the church bulletin, a series of tweets sent over a period of several weeks, a Skype or succinct video-conferencing class on the basics of the ministry of invitation can help to ease the awkwardness. The invitation does not need to be difficult. From just sharing information about work, school, or hobbies with a newcomer to the community or with friends at organizations with which you are affiliated, to stories about you or your family's church activities, it all opens the door for others to ask questions about *your* church. After the initial hello and welcome to the neighborhood, try an "I go to First Church. My family really likes it there. If you don't have a church, I'd be happy to have you join me sometime." It all seems so simple, but more often than not it is left unsaid. Simple training of the sales reps is an important part of successful church growth.

The Liturgy of Worship Welcome

Just as worship has a liturgical plan to follow, welcoming the stranger to worship should also have a strategic plan. Often we get only one chance to make the stranger a friend in Christ and potentially an active member in our church. A detailed plan of welcome is essential. There are five key stages in the worship welcoming process:

- *Setting the scene:* Make sure the entrance and vestibule areas to the sanctuary are welcoming and that any church information materials are clearly accessible. Have packets available for the children of visitors. This can help alleviate the parents' need to marshal their little ones; often first-time visitors will keep their children with them. Coordinate with the nursery volunteers the procedures for informing visitors about childcare. Make sure that technology used to welcome and inform is in good working order. Make sure that the sanctuary is prepared: pews and seats clean and orderly, visitors' materials in the pews or seating areas available and not dated. Make sure the general appearance of the sanctuary is warm and orderly. In larger sanctuaries, roping off pews or arranging seating so there is a comfortable-yet-full feeling is a good technique. Make certain there is a full complement of greeters and ushers in place who are knowledgeable about their roles; often a three-by-five card with general instructions is helpful in standardizing the procedures for these volunteers.
- *Welcoming during worship:* Have ways of identifiying visitors by using name tags, flowers, or friendship pads, for instance. Include words of welcome in any printed resources and a personal welcome from the worship leaders. Welcome statements should be well crafted so that the message is received in a few words. Occasionally a humorous disclaimer can be included. This will liberate everyone to become a welcoming presence: "Whether you are a first-time visitor or a fifty-year member, please accept our gracious

welcome even if we should have known who you are by now." Have assigned guest identifiers who, near the end of the worship service, plan their approach to personally welcome visitors. Depending on the ratio of visitors to guest identifiers, either the identifier should adopt the visitor or pass the visitor along to an active church family so that person can become a host for any after-church activities.

- *Getting from benediction to the bagels:* Make sure the coffee hour is attractively appointed and the food is varied enough for all tastes. If you want families to stick around, child-friendly foods are essential. Organize simple ways of connecting children who attended church school with their parents after worship. Devise a procedure for the pastor-to-parishioner pass-off of visitors. Create a space for church members' photos so that visitors can identify people they may know.
- *Following up:* Within the week, have some personal contact by phone or in person. This can be from the pastor or a church member or even a handwritten note. If a person or family does not return to worship for a month, then make a second personal "miss you" contact. Be persistent, not rude. You can either encourage another visit or gain information about the reasons for not attending. Even negative feedback can be helpful for welcoming future visitors or for program-development strategies.

Sacrament and Rite Evangelism

Sacrament and rite evangelism are closely related. Depending on the policies of the church, the sacrament of baptism and the rites of marriage and the funeral bring nonmembers—some who feel an affinity for the church and others who are complete strangers—to the church. In cases of baptism and marriage, presacrament counseling provides a significant church growth opportunity. In some churches, membership is required for receiving the sacrament of baptism or having a church wedding. The reality is that responsible and effective pastoral care follow-up carries with it an evangelism component. If we really show that the church cares, the recipient of that care will then care for the church.

Using the Media

The large, full-color holiday newspaper advertisement cost $500, and it was impressive. Pictures of individual church members of every age, ethnic, and racial background and every economic status were saying, "You have seen our majestic steeple! Why not come and meet the people under the steeple? A blessed Christmas to you from the steeple people." All the vital information about the church and its holiday service was also included. At the Sunday worship following this ad's appearance, a random but planned survey was taken of members and visitors in attendance. Of the sixteen visitors asked, none had come because of the "steeple people" ad. Only one had seen it. Of the thirty members surveyed, three had noticed it. This church advertised weekly in the local paper, and not one visitor had attended in response to the advertisement. Several came when there was a featured story about a special program or about one of the church's ministries. When it comes to spending on church growth activities, up-to-date websites and other tech media presences such as Facebook, Twitter, or local cable access are preferred. The print media should be the solution only when there is a potential feature story.

When using print or tech media, a church or staff member with exceptional writing skills is an important public relations asset. Often the secular media do not understand the polity or dynamics of parish ministry and, therefore, articles and stories will fall short in their reporting. Having an in-house writer makes it more likely that a well-written story will get the message properly conveyed. Having an in-house writer also allows quotes to be appropriate and accurate.

Technology is now the primary media for new member attraction. A plan for the use of technology should be well conceived and well planned. A detailed communication roadmap for the use of a website and social media is vital. Regardless of the size of a church's budget, a well-designed web presence is foundational to church growth. Training staff or church members to keep it current is also essential. One of the most creative ways to expand the church growth and evangelism ministry is to involve the whole congregation in using social media to share the church's story and ministries. Facebook friends and Twitter followers become potential participants in the life of the church. Encouraging members to tweet about sermons, church programs, and wider mission stories carries the church message to thousands of people outside the immediate church family.

Where to Place the Bouncy Castle and Where to Be Seen

The homecoming Sunday plans were progressing without a hitch. Now there was a major discussion about where to place the children's large inflatable bouncy castle and slide. The massive green lawn behind the church seemed to be the most appropriate area to situate these giant children's toys. But a counter-opinion was placed on the table: the smaller lawn in front of the church. The case was built on the premise that children don't care where they bounce, and besides, five roads converge in front of the church where there is a traffic light. Hundreds of cars will see that our church celebrates children. This second opinion of church growth thinking won the day. The corollary was established: "If it's an outdoor activity that would give good publicity for the church, and its location doesn't diminish the impact of the activity, then it's simple. The event should be held on the church campus in the place most visible to the public." We want our joy in God's love to be seen by the entire world.

Sometimes the creative use of church outdoor space can also be a way to introduce visitors to the church. If the church is located near a historic cemetery, then provide information for walking tours. Or why not build a community labyrinth or garden on church property? Offer resources for studying the ecological features of the church grounds. If the church's history ties into the history of the town or nation, receive informal historical recognition. Make sure to post all this on "things to see" websites and in print resources.

There is also the question of where to be seen in the community. This is particularly true for pastors and identified church leaders.

There are a limited number of hours in our schedules for non-church-related or even family-related activities. While personal and professional interests may dictate some of our community involvement time, there may be some choices that could be aimed at church growth. Our participation in educational, civic, service, and social organizations might be guided not only by our personal interests but also by the growth interests of the church.

Brokering the Building for Growth

Most churches will design and sponsor special programs, such as artistic performances, informative lectures and workshops, and vacation Bible schools all open to the public. Print materials about future programs and about the church should be visible and readily accessible to those nonmembers who are attending the event. Guests should be subtly surrounded by visual, audiovisual and spoken information about the church and its ministry.

Along with the community programs planned by the church, there are other ways of what could be called brokering the building for growth. Community organizations are often looking for meeting and performance space for their programs. Some may wish to rent space. Others may be willing to pay for the basic costs of maintenance and utilities. Still other nonprofits may want free space for their programs. Remember, all organizations bring visitors into church space and can be catalysts for at least a few people becoming interested in the church and its ministry. While seeking to be supportive of community organization space needs, the selection of those who use the building should be somewhat guided by their possible future benefit to the church.

One of the most effective church growth strategies is the designing of covenants and contracts with long-term nonprofit tenants. Let's be honest. Many of these long-term users want nothing to do with the church's ministry. They only want an inexpensive rental price. While wishing to be supportive of many needed outreach ministries, the church should also find ways to have closer ties with those organizations who share building space. Mutually beneficial covenants and contracts are tools that benefit everyone. Imagine a nonassociated preschool covenanting with the congregation. Church staff have visibility in their programs. They share information with the parents about the church's children's activities. They can develop parent and family programs together. Teachers can meet together with the pastor and other church leadership for mutual long-range planning, all in exchange for slightly lower rent. With the exception of groups like AA and NA, which require anonymity, closer ties for the mutual benefit of all should be established. If the goal of ministry is to extend the hand of fellowship to strangers so they'll then come to know the joy of following Christ, then the church building itself is a key resource for nurturing a vibrant and growing family of faith.

Going Out of the Box to Bring Them In

Who would have thought that the Super Bowl commercials would be as anticipated as the game itself? Who would have thought green talking lizards would sell insurance or an overweight dog would be the inspiration for buying a car? These outside-the-box commercials often draw the viewer in because of the joy or humor they offer. Why should the church not be in the business of putting a smile on a face or a laugh in the heart?

Now for what some of you may have been bewildered since the beginning of this chapter, namely, the clash between Colonial Americans and German engineering: the Volkswagen. The question is "How do you attract members of the community to a three-hundredth-anniversary celebration of a well-known community church?" The answer was simple. Dress members in Colonial garb and send them to the main shopping thoroughfare in town. Have them speak in modified Old English as if they were from 1705. Have them ask questions of downtown shoppers about the twenty-first-century things they notice around them. "What's that?" "That's an automobile. Terrific invention replacing the horse. It's a Volkswagen Bug!" "Sure doesn't look like it could pull a plow." After creating this odd scenario, have the actors invite people to church. Present people with an activities sheet done in Colonial-style lettering. No matter if it's in front of the local grocery store or the Volkswagen dealership, the sale has been made in a unique and whimsical manner. Try street performers, public art exhibits, cooking demonstrations of global foods, a hot-air balloon floating above the church campus with a banner trailing from it, Christmas festivals with Colonial Carolers, model train exhibits, crèche displays in the narthex, haunted steeple tours on Halloween. The sky should be the limit in spreading the word about a church that has the gifts of joy and the ability to laugh at itself. All it takes is a group of creative and willing members sitting down together and prayerfully and energetically brainstorming. The goal of bringing the joy of Christ to others in the community should be first. God will reveal the commercial endeavors that are pleasing in God's sight.

Call it evangelism, call it church growth, call it an attempt to fill the pews or meet the budget, if we believe we have Good News to share, we should be zealous in our efforts to bring friends and strangers into our church communities. We need to do what it takes "to go and make disciples of all people." (See Appendix E, Church Growth Checklist.)

Inspiration

"Note the turtle. He only gets ahead when he sticks his neck out."

—Anonymous

"Church is sacred space where saints and sinners gather to hear God's word. . . . There is no spiritual test to come in, no intellectual position to which one must agree. . . . This is the vision of the comprehensive church."

—Diana Butler Bass[1]

Prayer

God, send us out to invite them to the family table at which you sit with us. Let us never be timid in seeking to build a community of faith that reflects the diversity and unity of your realm. In Jesus' name. Amen.

12

Money Matters

Show Me Your Wallet, Show Me Your Faith

Body Building Exercises

- In the area of church finance and fundraising, what roles should the pastor play?
- What are the key theological constructs that underlie your understanding of financial stewardship?
- What guides your giving to the church and other service and wider mission organizations? Do you tithe? Why or why not?

It was a biennial event. It could have been at the kitchen table or around a church stewardship committee meeting table. In the midst of some discussion on financial giving to the church, he would take out his wallet and place it on the table saying: "Show me your faith!" It was a visual statement that proclaimed that God owns it all—even the money in our pockets—and trusting in God means we needn't trust in the Almighty Dollar. He learned that theological truth as he lived faithfully through the Great Depression and during a successful financial career. He was a man who said he was so thankful to God that he often doubled his tithe to his church and other social welfare and justice causes. The man with the wallet was my father. He was for me the model of Christian generosity in an often greedy society. He realized that everything is a gift from God and all was God's. He understood the concept of the stewardship guru Douglas John Hall that "stewardship is our human vocation!"[1]

Of the topics that we are told are taboo to speak of in public—money, sex, religion, and politics—money still seems to be the one spoken of in the most secretive terms. How odd when it is the most visible sign of power in today's society. The economy is built on it.

Money equals power. Crime and conflicts develop because of the lack of it or the disproportionate distribution of it. Our basic needs—food, clothing, and shelter—are linked to it! Corporations and political campaigns rely on it. Personal worth and esteem often linked to it. These are realities and the church needs to become more comfortable talking about money. Frequently the world's values and power-brokering systems are defined in financial terms. Since the church is in the business of defining personal worth, assets, and power through the lens of the Gospel, then it cannot keep silent on the place and use of money in its members' lives.

The basis for the church's speaking forthrightly about money and materialism is woven into the fabric of scripture. The Bible puts no positive or negative value on money. It does offer warnings that it can be assigned too high a priority in people's lives. Most will remember the story of the rich young ruler. It is a text that demands a creative spirit to fully understand. The rich young ruler comes to Jesus wanting to know what he must do to inherit eternal life. After passing the first test by doing all that the law commanded, Jesus then tells him to go and give away his money to the poor and in doing so he will have "treasure in heaven." The young man walks away disheartened because he cannot do what Jesus has asked. But consider what Jesus might have said if the young ruler had replied: "Okay! To whom shall I give it?" Knowing Jesus, he would probably have answered, "Keep your money, because I know you'll use it in the most righteous and gracious ways that God intended." The wealthy young ruler failed the "What is your god?" test. Paul's admonition to Timothy makes the issue of money crystal clear: "For the love of money is a root of all kinds of evil, and in their eagerness to be rich some have wandered away from the faith and pierced themselves with many pains" (1 Tim 6:10).

It is loving money more than we love God and neighbor that makes money and material possessions evil. In our world money is power, and the question that remains is whether that power is used for the good of me or in service to God. The first building block in matters of money is showing our love for God through our use of it.

There is another theological motive for giving that needs to be stressed if the spirit of Christian giving is to be fully experienced. We give out of thanksgiving, not out of guilt or as a way of purchasing eternal life. Our giving is a response to all that God has given to us. Because we have been blessed we want to praise God with our generosity. Helping others to see how blessed they are is an essential message that must be lifted up in the life of the church.

Another Bible-based building block is one that is difficult and even frightening to grasp. The earth and all that "dwells therein" is God's, not yours or mine. Everything we have is on loan to us. We own nothing. It is God's and therefore it is sacred. Believing this truth that was announced at creation, we understand that we are nothing more than tenders, like Adam and Eve, and stewards of God's property. So when it comes to money we do not spend as we please but spend as would please God. Church leaders need to be bold in addressing the issue of money and materialism so that the pains that do come with the love of money are avoided and so that we will find joy in pleasing God through our generosity. We must acknowledge that all we have been given is on loan to us for our time of tending God's world.

Our Roles in Dealing with Money Matters

Even if we are not schooled in abilities to understand the intricacies of finance, there are important roles we are called to play for the spiritual health of the church and its members. The money needed for the success of church programs, buildings, and mission becomes our concern.

As has been alluded to already, we are to be the go-to person for teaching the Biblical concept of stewardship. It may happen in a sermon, but equally important is our teaching in small groups and with governing and other leadership boards and committees. While some pastors incorrectly believe that money issues should be left to lay leaders, we need to take a key role in preparing and selecting the themes and media resources for church financial stewardship and capital campaign activities. If left to lay leaders alone, often in finance-related professions, who believe they understand money matters better than we do, the raising and spending of money will often lack the faith dimension unique to church. We need to be involved in training those who solicit financial gifts. Again, we do not want our approach to have merely a secular tone in its presentation. We take a leadership role because we are to live by faith, even when it comes to finance. We believe that our faith and our wallets are intertwined.

During budget planning we need to be a key player because we see the whole picture and can bring objectivity to the budget building process. We spend all our time stewarding the church's ministries and have considerable knowledge of its financial needs in all areas of ministry. We also have a more than passing notion of what the whole membership holds as priorities for the church's ministry. The chair of the buildings and grounds committee is primarily looking at building-and-ground needs. Christian education, wider mission, worship and music committee leaders know the priorities for spending in their corners of the world. Whether we relish the responsibility or not, how the budget is finalized shapes the program we must lead and, yes, are held accountable for. Faithful and empowering ministry requires diligent attention when budgets are being prepared. It is good to get ahead of the curve by presenting early a suggested budget. Numbers alone won't sell the budget. It needs to be practically and theologically sound for serious reflection and subsequent discussion. We can leave the ingathering, financial tracking, and investment strategy to others. But to leave budget planning to others is done only at the risk of our own peril.

It was time for the October treasurer's report at the monthly all-boards meeting. Since it was near the year's end he thought he'd give an update with final projections. "I'm concerned that we'll have a $40,000 deficit!" Now into the midst of the joy the board members had been experiencing in light of increasing vitality in the church came an unnecessary injection of fear. There was a sudden sense of overwhelming concern and confusion. The pastor was uncomfortable because she wasn't quite sure how to offer the actual financial reality. She cautiously asked to be recognized. Prayerfully she shaped her pastoral counsel: "We should applaud Fred's good work in making sure we are fiscally solvent. But we shouldn't feel too concerned right now, because I believe about $65,000 of annual giving will come at year end. We know the members who are behind on their giving, and there's no reason to believe they won't honor their pledge. We are a blessed church to have such generosity." We pastors need to be a pivotal resource when it comes to giving patterns and budgetary requirements. Volunteer church leaders will have their terms of office and the dynamics of church finance will all be new to those who follow. Most churches follow this pattern of high giving at the beginning of the calendar year. This results from prepaid gifts and from others who choose to make larger year-end contributions. The calendar of holy days will influence the month-to-month giving. The end of summer will usually result in a renewed stream of exceptional generosity. There are also the realities that our pastoral-care ministries bring to the scene: some will feel blessed by that ministry and give more of their treasure to the church, and others may fall on hard times and be unable to be as generous as they would like. Church giving is not an exact science. Whether we feel comfortable with the role or not, we are called to have the basic knowledge of our particular church's solicitation styles and giving trends. While some would hesitate to know the actual gifts of church members, pastors might wish to at least have some information about these gifts. Knowing is an asset in budget planning and in identifying potential pastoral-care issues. It also allows the pastor and lay financial leaders to join in viewing money as an issue of faith.

During our ministry we will probably play a role in more than three dozen financial stewardship campaigns. That's right—more than thirty-six occasions of asking for gifts of time, talent, and treasure. We will learn about the generosity and frugality of the faithful. We will celebrate and we will agonize. Truth be told, most of the laity called (or begged) to lead the annual stewardship campaign will lead such an effort fewer than two or three times in their lives. Some stewardship campaign chairs may have fundraising experience with other nonprofits, but that will probably be rare. While some chairs of the effort may be skilled in fundraising and able to work cooperatively with the professional leadership, most will have only a cursory knowledge in the basics of Christian stewardship and fundraising. We must be instructors in the basics of church fundraising. There are ample resources to assist us. But we will need to be the ones who know the fundamentals and often the prodders of the campaign leadership. Having a basic outline of the steps that need to be followed is often the difference between a bountiful harvest and a weak investment.

An Heiress

> On one occasion, the words seemed to get stuck in my throat. There she sat, an heiress to a prominent hi-tech conglomerate fortune, enjoying her club sandwich. She was not a very active member of the church, but I had come to know her when I had been a pastoral presence during some rough times that involved her health and her marriage. My mind was jumbled. "Say something! Now is the time to ask. You can do it. Come on!" After a few random comments about some church building and program needs I began to explain our major capital campaign goals. Finally the time came for the words that needed to be given voice: "We were thinking you might contribute at least $100,000 toward the $1.5 million goal." She paused and said, "I've never given more than $3,000 in any one year to any organization." I was now feeling empowered: "Well, there's always a first time!" After lunch I paid the $32.95 tab and would wait two more days to learn that I actually left the restaurant with a net gain of $29,967.05. Her $30,000 gift was ten times what she had given to any other organization in one year in her whole life.

It was then I realized it doesn't hurt to ask. When it is done in faith and with a pastoral style, God will provide more than we would ever expect. Sometimes we'll have to be hands-on fundraisers. This may be because we are the only ones with whom a potential donor has a link to the church. We may be one of the few in the church who can call them by name and know their ability to give. Or we have had a special relationship because we have been their pastor in joy and in sorrow, in sickness and in health. The privilege of asking for a financial commitment is nothing more than an extension of our asking for a commitment to follow in Christ's footsteps. When it comes to faith, maybe the most significant commitment we can call for involves the wallet.

Financial Stewardship Campaign Basics—From Pocket to Program

There is an overused expression: “We have all the money we need for the ministry of the church; it’s in our pockets.” A well-planned, organized, and impassioned financial stewardship campaign can raise all the money that is needed. There are an abundance of resources that can be purchased. These will walk leadership through the fundraising plan. Here’s a detailed plan that can lead to spiritual growth within the church, as well as garner the necessary financial resources for vital church program ministry:

- Schedule an initial meeting of campaign leaders three months before the beginning of the actual program.
    - Discuss the biblical foundations for the stewardship of time, talent, and treasure and the historic and modern tithe.
    - Consider options for giving, including e-giving.
    - Establish the theme: make it biblical; make it personal.
    - Prepare the calendar.
- Solicit hopes and dreams as well as the actual costs to implement those hopes and dreams,
    - from the congregation.
    - from the committees and staff.
- Build a budget reflecting the dreams and actual costs. Include all sources of income: weekly offering, pledges, special gifts and funds, endowment income, rental income, second-mile giving.
- Prepare the communications flow for:
    - Initial Communications
        - snail mail, since all members are not tech literate (but don’t overlook e-mail)
        - a giving challenge to step up to a tithe or increase by a certain percentage, moving toward a tithe

- A Narrative Budget
    - broken down by program areas (such as worship, pastoral care, faith development), including costs for salaries and benefits, and property maintenance
    - shows costs per member for individual programs, such as costs of curriculum, staff time, utilities, and maintenance per child in church school per year
    - See Appendix F, A Sample Narrative Budget; this is a helpful worksheet.
- Detailed Communications
    - newsletter conveying information, laity testimonies as to why they give, information from committees about how they steward the money they receive
    - bulletin inserts or audiovisuals in and around the worship service
    - communications with children and youth programs
    - personal stories—"Why I Give?"—in worship
    - time at meetings and gatherings to discuss the narrative budget
    - open meetings with members; while often poorly attended, these allow for new program ideas to be expressed and demonstrate to everyone that this is an open process

◆ Prepare a second all-church communication that includes:

- an introductory letter, containing
    - encouragement to step up toward a tithe or to tithe
    - reintroduction of the theme
    - pledge reception timeline
    - information about dedication and ingathering worship

- Pledge Card
  - ∗ either generic or with a suggested gift option (Example: You gave X last year; if you increase by $1, $5, $10 per week, it would be Y)
  - ∗ showing payment options, including electronic transfer, credit card, securities
  - ∗ a pledge of time and talent to the church, either as part of the formal stewardship campaign or as a way of introducing sacrificial giving
  - ∗ decision devotionals to help givers center in on the spiritual nature of their gift

◆ Gather and train disciples or solicitors (whatever we call them, this is asking for Caesar's money for God's use) equipped with:

- training resources and script for contact
- names of potential givers closely matched with their callers
- resources for gathering from those who are contacted their hopes and dreams and pastoral concerns; encourage callers to be positive and help them to be able to say: "I give to our church because . . ." and "Won't you step up with me?"
- pastor's guidance for dealing with persons and families who might be difficult to deal with or who are facing health or financial struggles

◆ Prepare leaders' gifts and pre-mailing contacts.

- Ask the leaders to set an example by making their commitment prior to the church-wide stewardship campaign. All those callers who will contact the broader church constituency should be encouraged to make their commitments; sharing the total amount they have given can add momentum for others to give generously.

  - Before making contact by mail (to as many people as possible and preferably to the whole church), make contact in person or by phone. Share the story; encourage increasing the gift; give the timing for the ingathering.
  - Don't forget the nonmember but affiliated people. Solicit from nonmembers who are involved in the church but are not on mailing lists: community youth in church programs, choir members, individuals who are unchurched but consider the congregation their home for spiritual growth and social and mission activities.

- Plan the Dedication or Ingathering Sunday. Make this Sunday a festival with as many groups participating as possible. It should be a celebration of the whole church. Be sure to include elements in the service that are attractive to families as well as long-term members.
- Follow up. This is crucial. The difference between a budget that strengthens the church and one that impedes its ministry is often what is gathered in the one to three months following the ingathering Sunday. Persistence is the operative word; remember the friend at midnight or the widow before the judge in scripture. The motto is "I will be contacting you until you make a pledge or tell me no!"
- Make tough decisions. If the gifts are insufficient to meet the budget, serious questions need to be addressed:
  - Do we go on faith with the presented budget?
  - Do we consider a second effort or do we plan special fundraising activities?
  - Do we cut the budget? If cuts are made, the rationale should include cutting an equal percentage from each section of the budget. Too often salaries and benefits and wider mission take the brunt of the cost cutting. Pain should be equally shared.

- At the conclusion, wrap up the campaign with:
  - a church-wide letter of appreciation to all who gave. A handwritten personal note from the finance chair or even the pastor adds a distinctive dimension to the general "thank you" communication.
  - a system for reporting gifts at intervals (quarterly, semi-annually), using the bulletin, e-mail, website.
  - non-finance-related contact six-months after the campaign coordinated by the year-round stewardship committee. These calls say that the person is more than his or her financial gift to the church. The tone should be pastoral.

Those of us who choose to excuse ourselves from dealing with church finance and stewardship issues will pay the price for our absence. An effective annual stewardship campaign and faith-built budget do require our attention.

When things fall apart and dreams come alive, we might have the privilege of taking a leadership role in what many parish clergy would rather avoid: a capital campaign. It is now time to show me your faith and to show me your portfolio. Pray for a bountiful harvest and keep those faithful wallets open.

Inspiration

"Just like in the early church, the churches should have no poor among them. Its rich will have learned to recite the . . . prayer—God, help me to handle possessions with a light touch—and to live a life where not the one with the most toys wins, but the one who bounces his or her last check (in sharing) wins." —Leonard Sweet[2]

Prayer

Help me to proclaim a Gospel that says that the truly rich are those who invest in the spiritual capital revealed to us in your supreme investment in our salvation, Jesus Christ. Take my life, my spiritual and material assets, and let it be lived in praise to thee. Amen.

13

The Capital Campaign

When Things Fall Apart and Dreams Come Alive

Body Building Exercises

- As a pastor or church leader, what are your initial thoughts when you hear the words "capital campaign"?
- If your church needs to have a capital campaign, what do you see your involvement to be in the effort?
- How can a capital campaign be a faith-strengthening activity?

The roof is leaking and the paint is peeling; the sanctuary looks shabby; the stained glass is covered with exhaust smoke from the nearby highway; there's a need for more creative children's programs because of a growing community with young families; emergency calls for financial help to impoverished hurricane-devastated countries arrive unexpectedly. We all have received the call from our alma maters, our clubs, our charities for capital campaign commitments. These institutions repeat the solicitations approximately every ten years. It's no different with the local church. Eventually there are major projects that the annual budget cannot sustain or opportunities for creative programs that will be missed because of the lack of financial resources. These will require a major fundraising effort from church members and the wider community.

When is the right time for a major financial effort in the life of a local parish? The answer is simple: when the building is in need of repair and refurbishing and when the dreams of a dynamic ministry are passionately calling. There will become an obvious tipping point when multiple capital needs can be put off no longer and when visions for exciting future ministries cannot be shelved for yet one more year.

The need will arise in both good and bad economic times. Just when the stock market is unstable, the wooden steeple will become unstable and become a danger to the church community. The stone exterior of the church will require repointing during a year of high unemployment. An influx of young families will arrive in the community, and refurbishing the church school and hiring staff to create attractive children's and youth ministry programs will be crucial. At the same time, some of the most generous givers will be moving out of the area. While slight adjustments can be made to timing, usually the best analysis calls for the time to be now. The decision is often a matter of adding up the needs and presenting the obvious to the family of faith.

1 The heating system often breaks down in the winter.

+1 The hymnals are falling apart and presenting visitors with a negative impression of the church.

+1 Families are leaving the church because the education wing is in disrepair and the program is unappealing.

+1 The organ pipes are aging and in need of revoicing and in some cases replacing.

+1 The church parking lot is potholed.

+1 The salaries for staff keep getting cut and staff are coming and going.

+1 A wider opportunity which could revitalize the church's mission ministry has a price tag the church cannot afford.

Add them up = Capital Campaign

Faith is about risking, going out not knowing, as Abraham and Sarah did, believing that God would provide what is needed and would bless them. The blessing can be reached if all give in proportion to their own thankfulness. Capital campaigns require reaching beyond annual giving and boldly making one-time gifts, usually from personal assets rather than annual income. Capital campaigns are one of the most visible signs of the depth of one's faith.

Do we need a hired hand? That is one of the first questions to be addressed in the decision-making process for a major campaign. There are many faith-based, credible fundraising organizations ready and willing to help—for a fair fee. In the majority of larger need cases, it is beneficial to consider employing them at least for the decision-making stages of the campaign. They play multiple roles in the implementation and successful completion of a major fund drive. They strengthen the fundraising effort by:

- helping to make the go or no-go decision as well as analyzing the scope and scale of the campaign.
- providing a broad base of biblical and theological insights that are often overlooked.
- bringing the basic knowledge of the "how tos."
- inspiring and prodding the leadership to carry out their responsibilities. ("They are being paid, so we had better not waste our money with inaction.")
- becoming the scapegoat when a few members become disenchanted with the fundraising process.
- keeping the follow-up process on track so the solicitation and receipts are completed in a timely manner.

Promo Video

The New York City network weatherman stood in the top of the bell tower of the massive Gothic church. In the distance the sun was rising over Long Island Sound. The sole cameraman was clinging to a railing so he could stabilize the picture. They were shooting the closing scene of a capital campaign promotional video. "In the three-hundred-year history of our church, God has given us some beautiful sunshine-filled days. We have also had our share of stormy weather when we lost our way. As I look out over the Sound, the sun is rising and I'm predicting a successful Looking to the Future campaign. I predict that our church will have many days filled with the light of God and the warmth of God's Spirit. Join me in giving sacrificially." Music up. Camera pan to the sunrise over the water. Cut! It was a take. The raw footage of the primary promotional resource for the campaign effort was complete. Now the editor was to work his technological magic and take several hours of videotape and edit it into a twelve-minute promotional piece for use at fundraising gatherings.

Books and consultants will enlighten those who venture out into the world of capital campaigns. The story of the weatherman in the tower highlights some of the efforts needed in developing a successful capital campaign:

- Select a theme that looks both to the past and to the future. This allows those who have an appreciation for the church's history, as well as those who have only a brief history, to join in their support of the campaign's goals.
- Provide a prominent theological undertone. Faith needs to be the cornerstone. Whether in promotional materials or through special devotional resources, there needs to be a scriptural underpinning.
- Devote plenty of time for planning after the initial commitment to a campaign. All facets must be well researched and well done. Take for example, writing the script, shooting the footage, and editing the raw film of the complete promotional video in the above example took three to four months. There are no shortcuts to thoroughness.
- The economic and cultural circumstances of the congregation should be considered when choosing the campaign's tone.
- Everyone needs to feel included. In the promotional video were distinct sections that allowed everyone to find something they wanted for their church. Scenes of church activities included a cross-section of every facet of the ministry. Some may give because they want a new boiler and others may give because they believe

in creating a fund to provide grants for innovative social outreach programs.

- Give sacrificially. The motto is not equal gifts but equal sacrifice. A key element in reaching the goal is addressing an issue that no one usually wants to broach: What is the giving potential of each member of the church? A broad-based committee needs to meet in confidence and decide what is an equitable sacrifice for each member. Pairing people of reasonably equal financial worth for the personal solicitation effort is important. In those private discussions, income and assets will be an open topic for discussion. In spite of being the spiritual head of the church, the pastor often needs to be present so the tone of the discussion is compassionate and sensitive to each member's ability to give.
- The best advice for the pastor is to be joyous and affirming of the campaign's goals. This is no time for gloom. Be ready to give your equally sacrificial gift. Be humble when the feedback comes that your ministry is the inspiration for members' generosity. Be prayerful and strong when the few who are not your biggest fans get their chance to openly offer their feelings about the church.

Some of the most fulfilling days of ministry can be times when the financial need is great. It's a time when dreams and visions may be put into action. It's a time when the call to sacrificial giving can bring out the depth of a church member's faith. It's a time when we who say we believe in sacrificial giving are called to put our best efforts and money forward as witness to those beliefs. It's also a time when our pastoral skills will be supremely tested. We should not retreat from being the spiritual leader of these efforts to renew and revitalize the churches we serve.

When we challenge our members to tie their faith and their wallets and portfolios together, we will make a life that is filled with the joy of God. The rich young ruler forfeited the peace and joy that comes with generosity when he made his money his god. Let us not go and do likewise.

Inspiration

There is a story told about John Wesley's famous three-liner: ""Make all that you can! Save all that you can! Give all that you can!" Reportedly one person in the congregation shouted "Amen!" after the first two exhortations. However, the response to the third exhortation was "What a way to spoil a good sermon." How about an "Amen!" when it comes to sacrificial giving?

Prayer

Ever-giving God, we have been blessed by an abundant outpouring of your generosity. Challenge us to show our faith by laying everything we have on the line so that others might take the risk of foolish, yet faithful, sharing. Make us never timid in asking "What is your god?" to those who are tempted by greed. In the name of the One who gave it all for our sake. Amen.

14

Touch and Tech

Emerging Partners in Getting the Good News Out

Body Building Exercises

- How do you feel about the nonstop emergence of more and more communications technology?
- What do you see to be the upside of this technology in the local church's ministry?
- What are the challenges it presents to you as a leader in a local church?
- Thinking creatively, consider a few ways to use technology for the enhancement of your church's ministry.

The Jones family (George, forty-five, Jenny, forty-four, and Abigail, ten) enter the sanctuary doors, and communication technology enables a welcome message, tailored specifically to them, to appear on their smartphone screens: "Welcome to Christ Church, George and Jenny. If Abigail is with you today, there is Sunday School this morning, as well as youth group this afternoon." Below the welcome message is an electronic bulletin, detailing the order of worship for the service (no more paper). If Abigail decides to remain in worship, her mobile device will automatically display numerous Bible-themed games and puzzles to help keep her attention during the service. In the sanctuary, a large video projection shows pictures of recent activities at the church, which were uploaded to cloud storage when they were taken and are displayed automatically. On an opposite wall, a live video feed is being broadcast from a missionary in South Africa who is answering questions and speaking about her experience. A third screen connects the congregation with the home of a shut-in family who is unable to attend worship in person. They can see and hear everything that happens in the service. As people gather, congregants can use their mobile devices to send prayer requests to the prayer leader, which will then be mentioned during prayer time.

The service begins. During times of musical participation the words to the song being sung appear on one of the screens. Those more musically inclined can click a link on their mobile device to view the actual music, and not just the words. When scripture lessons are read, the verse being read is automatically sent to the mobile devices of the congregation. During the sermon, congregants tweet questions and comments about what they hear, which the minister can see and—sometimes—chooses to answer or address right on the spot. At the end of the service, congregants are given the option to instantly save a digital copy of the sermon to their mobile device, or to send a link to others, who might have been unable to attend. Mobile devices monitor who you have been close to in previous fellowship time, and, in communication with the church network, send an alert if those same people are present at worship: "Jan and Glenn Smith are here today, if you'd like to say hello."[1]

This tech vision of the church of the future by a colleague has a surreal feel to it. Yet this future is not all that distant and not all that surreal to the next generation of worshippers. The capacity of technology to enhance ministry should not be overlooked. Embedded within the vision are some very attractive and creative concepts for the advancement of ministries of inclusion, evangelism, faith development, mission education, and worship. We need to employ the new to enhance the message without technology becoming the message. We ought to consider it a highly valued resource for getting the message out that God became flesh and called all people to become part of a close-knit community of love. Smartphones, tablets, and other current and emerging technologies can bring us closer together into community, provided we take care that they do not unknowingly create a second-hand intimacy running counter to the depth of community of which the Gospel speaks.

While this chapter will offer some implementable uses for technology, a disclaimer is needed. If the primary purpose of this chapter were only to offer such suggestions, it would soon be outdated. This chapter will attempt to wrap the creative use of the emerging technologies within a philosophical, might we say theological, framework.

The Christmas narrative in John's Gospel (yes, there is one) is simple and profound: "And the Word became flesh and dwelt among us." Incarnation: God comes in a human body, in Jesus Christ. He is the one who ate and drank in bodily form with saints and sinners, who healed with the touch of flesh on flesh. John's concise incarnation narrative has been the core principle of the church's ministry since its inception: Being in the presence of others and touching others so they know they are not alone on this miraculous, God-given journey called life, this is at the heart of the ministry of the Christian church. The church should be a place where we touch and get in touch with others. Being physically present with other journeying Christians cannot be replaced by tweeting or texting the message.

All who believe in incarnation-based theology should look at the emergence of communication technology and social networking with an eager yet analytical spirit. I embrace much of what technology has to offer. In the infancy of cable TV, I wrote and produced local faith-based programs. I also worked with a computer programmer to create some of the first "church history" gaming and designed a plan and raised money for a TV production studio in two churches I served. With a colleague I helped conceive a church youth center that had a video-gaming component. I have used editing capabilities to integrate movies into my sermons. While I may not be fully tech savvy, I do have a laptop, an Android phone with many, many apps, a tablet, and multiple e-mail accounts. I blog, tweet, text, and Skype. I am on Facebook and LinkedIn. I have encouraged technology-tied members of my church to tweet about my sermons during worship. But in spite of all of this, there is a lingering whisper in my soul: "And the Word became flesh." Being present in the flesh is central to being the church of Jesus Christ. With all of this technology, still my primary modes of communication are in person visitation and the phone.

The point is this: While not denigrating "high-touch" ministry a bit, we must recognize we live in a world that is always connected, and if the church wants to remain relevant, we need to make technology an ally, not an adversary. To the general public, Apple has no connection to the Garden of Eden tree of knowledge (even "apple" is a misinterpretation of the fruit on the tree). "The Cloud," the digitized storage place for vast quantities of information, is rarely perceived as the place from where the messianic Savior will arrive.

How to partner high touch with high tech is tricky business. My wife's lifelong profession has been reference librarian (now called knowledge and learning specialist). If there is any place where technology and customer service has been significantly affected it is in the public library. My wife's role has changed from leading people to the perfect books to helping people discern the most trusted and scholarly resources found on the Internet. Because so many people rely solely on Google and other search engines for information gathering, there is a steadily growing decrease in personal, face-to-face library customer service. Human interaction and in-person discussions on issues are slowly disappearing. For some there is a subtle grieving. More and more research affirms the pain of the replacement of the high touch by high tech. If you're not convinced, think back to your last few phone encounters with a company's customer service department. How many times have you wanted to cry out, "I just want to talk to a human being!"

When you are partnering high touch and high tech, consider that the church needs to establish a hierarchy of communication resources.

- *In person:* Regardless of the parishioner's age, most people want to have a pastor who knows them and calls them by name. Whether it's in teaching or evangelization, nothing has a more profound effect than an incarnate encounter.
- *By telephone:* A spoken word adds depth. Inflection and symmetry enhance understanding. Clarity can be obtained with a back-and-forth conversation.
- *By written personal word:* A note carries with it a special feeling that I cared enough to think about the words I am sending you and

took the time to be thoughtful and sensitive while writing. Who doesn't love to find a personal letter in the mailbox?

- *By visual tech tools such as Skype:* Seeing the speaker enhances the communication experience and, of course, we can connect for study, business, or planning. Geography is no longer an impediment to being together.
- *By e-mail and texting:* These can be used for quick and efficient sharing.
- *By social networking*: Facebook, LinkedIn, blogs, and church websites, while not being the best tools for true community building, can disseminate information to the larger communities in which we work and live.
- *By the printed word for mass distribution:* There are published paper resources still valuable to the committed, such as the Sunday worship bulletin and the monthly newsletter. Of course with increasing advances in high resolution digital display technology and the mass acceptance of electronic hand-held devices, the printed word on paper may soon have very limited use.

How is it possible to determine which technological resource or combination of resources to use? This is not always apparent and can require more examination.

- Is the communication for an individual, a select smaller group or target audience, the church community at large, or an even wider community?
- Is the reason for the communication pastoral, faith development, church growth, administrative, or general in nature?
- If the mailing reaches individuals and smaller audiences, what is the level of the individual's or group's access to the technology and their comfort in using it?
- If we choose the largest audience possible, how do we attractively present all we want to share?

- How do we discern what should be shared, and how do we select our words and images so that the message is clear and benefits the church's mission? How can we be sure that confidences are not broken? The world is watching. Things could "go viral."

Frequently a combination of all these touch and tech tools will be essential. A very clear example of this comes from pastoral care. At the time of a death and during the following bereavement period, we almost unknowingly employ multiple touch and tech resources. Upon being notified of a death, we immediately telephone the family of the person who has died. We then reach out to touch through our pastoral visits. The church's secretary or administrative assistant shares the news with the church family by the printed Sunday bulletin, on the website, and through e-mail. Using electronic calendar alerts, our pastoral-care ministry is enhanced by our being reminded on a one-month, three-month, six-month and one-year anniversary of the death. This information permits us to set up home visits, phone calls, or e-mails. To blend touch with tech, many of us notify trained lay caregivers to keep contact with surviving family members. In most ministries of pastoral care, a constant element of high touch is paramount.

The key to the effective balance between touch and tech is a knowledge of church members' personalities, technological expertise, and lifestyles. Along with the general information gathered from interactions in church settings, inquiries about people's communication resource preferences are useful. Many churches publish an annual directory. The inclusion of e-mail addresses, Facebook accounts, and so on, can help to ascertain the best forms of communication. "How would you like the church to communicate with you?" needs to be asked. Well-designed church websites and digital online church directories need to become the rule, not the exception. For a relevant and healthy church, as much visibility as possible on social networks is essential. While some small-membership churches may find the initial technology upgrade costs prohibitive, tech-savvy parishioners and the decreasing cost of hardware and software allows a church of almost any size to participate.

As seen in the opening story about Christ Church, technology can be a valuable, even indispensable tool in every aspect of ministry. Following are some basic ideas to stimulate your creative thinking.

- *Pastoral care:* Make quick, meaningful contacts through e-mail and social media; post care devotions for people facing illness and other personal health and relational challenges; bring homebound members into church-school classrooms to interact with children through Skype and other video conferencing resources.
- *Worship:* Create well-produced and faith-based multimedia presentations; expand music and instrumentation through digitalization; encourage worshippers to use hand-held devices to follow along in the reading of scripture, as well as to take notes as the sermon is preached.
- *Faith development:* Encourage dialogue on scripture and ethical issues, and share information through tweets and blogs; turn the youths' love of gaming into a way of discussing faith-based values; identify apps that can be used for personal study and devotion.
- *Wider mission:* Make real-time contact with people serving in the mission field or members at church work camps; offer ways of signing up for church, community, and wider mission opportunities online; create dialogue on advocacy issues by providing credible websites to visit.
- *Administration:* Collect and track donations; track interests and opportunities for volunteers; compile member and family histories so that they're easily retrievable.
- *Evangelism:* Have an attractive and welcoming presence on the major social media; explore other websites where you might want to have a presence or web connection; track and contact visitors.

The possibilities for the use of technology in ministry are beyond our comprehension. For the emerging generation of new church members, technology is second nature. Just as the invention of the printing press changed the norms for ministry hundreds of years ago, technology is reshaping the way the church delivers the Gospel message.

With technology woven into our everyday life, and with the enchantment that it brings to many, a few precautions need to be remembered:

- Design and use tech resources carefully. A poorly designed or out-of-date webpage is detrimental to the church's image. Multimedia-laden worship which is poorly coordinated and produced can be a turn-off to members and visitors.
- Consider the source. The Internet has opened the ability to share globally what an individual or group wants to share regardless of philosophical presumptions. A local university or seminary library has trained professionals who know the most responsible websites for research.
- Go global—Beware! Beware of announcing a hospitalization that was meant to be private or publishing a strident opinion that could be hurtful or demeaning. Beware and be vigilant, because the world is watching.
- Respond quickly. We heighten expectations when we frequently tweet or e-mail. Often we can feel like communications technology is using us rather than that we are using it. Dozens of voicemails, dozens of e-mails, handwritten sticky notes, and numerous other forms of written requests seeking pastoral care, administrative and program development information—the requests are endless. Add blog maintenance and promptness in texting and tweeting. Technology has heightened the myth of instant access. Instant access can be managed using these steps:
    - Design a workable plan for how and when the pastor will respond to the communication overload.
    - Obtain support for the plan from the church governing board.
    - Communicate the plan to all church members and others in the wider community who are in partnership with the church.
    - Be consistent with the plan.

- Establish a technology-response block of time each day and make the congregation aware of it.
- Place crisis as the number-one priority

Let us return to the touch-tech dilemma. In a *New York Times* article, Sherry Turkle, a psychologist and professor at MIT, provides great clarity regarding what is really important. She is the author of *Alone Together: Why We Expect More from Technology and Less from Each Other*. The essence of her article hits home because so many people feel disconnected because tech has replaced face-to-face communication. Professor Turkle's premise is that while we can be connected by technology, there remains a lack of real intimacy in these forms of communication. She writes: "We are tempted to think that our little "sips" of online connection add up to a big gulp of real conversation. But they don't. E-mail, Twitter, Facebook, all of these have their places—in politics, commerce, romance and friendship. But no matter how valuable, they do not substitute for conversation. . . . Face-to-face conversation unfolds slowly. It teaches patience. . . . We expect more from technology and less from each other." She also laments the loss of our ability to appreciate solitude. "We think constant connection will make us less lonely. The opposite is true. If we are unable to be alone, we are far more likely to be lonely. If we don't teach our children to be alone, they will only know how to be lonely."[2] We need to teach the world to model Christ's need for alone time by calling for technology-free space and time. We need to challenge the world to occasionally shut down secondhand forms of communication and experience intimacy firsthand. Remember our ministry's motto: "And the Word became flesh." It is our calling to share that message through every resource possible.

In a tech and touch world, the Jones family walks into church and a voice from above says, "Welcome Jenny and George and Abigail!" They are informed of the special day that lies ahead for them at church. Bill and Martha Smith, the greeters for the day, welcome the Jones family with handshakes and hugs and say, "We're so glad you're here!" The Jones family feel informed and warmed. They say, "We are so blessed to be here. Thanks be to God!"

Inspiration

"Despite the fact that we're territorial creatures who move through the world like small principalities, contact warms us even without knowing it. It probably reminds us of a time, long before deadlines and banks, when our mothers cradled us and we were enthralled and felt perfectly loved." —DIANE ACKERMAN[3]

Prayer

God, you who are as close to us as breathing and came close to us in Jesus Christ, give us the wisdom to learn how to keep in touch with those in need of your love. We give you thanks for the creative minds who have opened up a communication network that expands our reach to care for friends and strangers alike and helps us to gain a deeper knowledge of you. We also thank you for those mystics who challenge us to step aside and find a solitary, sacred time to listen for the whispers of your Spirit speaking. Amen.

15

Keeping the Jar Open—Praying and Playing

Body Building Leaders Stay Strong and Healthy amid the Challenges of Ministry

Body Building Exercises

- Besides parish ministry, what brings you the most joy?
- If you couldn't be a parish minister, what would you do for a living?
- If you weren't reading this most insightful book and if you didn't want to "do church," what would you do right now?

There are those moments in life when you say, "I wish I had thought of that!" For me, one of those moments happened in a continuing education setting. We were asked to write our own "realm of God" parable and then present it to our small group. Here's one that caught me off guard and offered a profound insight into life: "The realm of God is like the man who went out on a warm summer night to catch fireflies in a jar. But when he saw their lights flickering against the starlit black night sky he threw down his jar, fell on the ground, looked at the night sky, and began to laugh."

In the context of this book, the fireflies are the many calls of ministry that come upon us and constantly encircle us. The jar is our propensity to strive to get all of those ministry demands under control, to trap them and put a lid on so we feel we have command of them. And often when we focus our entire attention on keeping things under control, our soul becomes suffocated because it is locked up in an airtight prison of our own making. While some of us take our constant go, go, go ministry as a badge of honor, it just might be the reason we find ourselves gasping for our spiritual breath.

This concluding chapter of the book will be briefer, because we need to stop learning about doing ministry and start to just be. We need to take a break from being in the presence of God in our ministry and instead be in the presence of God by being outside of church activities. We need to step aside from paying attention to the church and pay attention to our spiritual health and our family health.

It starts with the 80-percent/20-percent rule that was highlighted at the beginning of the book. Remember, 80 percent of life is actually humorous and should be lived with some levity, while 20 percent is to be taken with full seriousness. We do sometimes take ourselves too seriously. Believing that we can save the world with just one more job completed, or one more visit or sermon will eventually snatch the joy from both our ministry and our lives.

We need a little praying time. We need a little playing time. There is an intersection between these two. Play—engaging in an activity for enjoyment and recreation rather than a serious or practical purpose—is a form of prayer we can offer God. Play is a psalm of praise and thanksgiving. Our smiles, our laughter, our spiritual *joie de vivre* are music to God's heart. An "ah" when we watch a sunset is a prayer that echoes throughout the heavens. Laughter at a humorous story binds us closely to God's Spirit. When we embrace and kiss a loved one, we experience the warmth of God's love. Play, just being, is our prayer of unutterable joy! We need this open jar time to help us attend to all facets of our health:

- physical
- family
- vocational
- spiritual and emotional
- relational
- avocational

We have chosen a profession that allows us to recreate as we do the job. For the compulsive, obsessive, task-oriented, there are "being" activities that can be included in doing the ministry job. Here are but a few ideas to muse on:

- Plan to have a church sports team, and play on it.
- Write a poem that might be published in a church devotional. Write new hymn words using the meter of a well-known hymn.
- Take a photograph, paint a picture, plan an art show.
- Attend a movie because it might be great sermon material.
- As a form of church growth strategy, consider taking a walk and greeting people along the way.
- Research the plant life on the church campus, design signs, and map a nature trail.
- Meditate on God's presence just by looking out your office window.
- Go into the sanctuary and play any kind of music you'd like on the piano or organ.
- Call homebound members and take a drive with them to a park, garden nursery, or other outdoor venue.
- With a group from your church, design and build a simple labyrinth. When you're stressed, walk it.
- Plant a church garden for the beautification of the campus or to grow vegetables for a local food pantry.
- Take continuing education courses, learning new skills in areas of your interests that would seem to have little to do with ministry, technology, art, or sports officiating. If you are questioned about its efficacy, be creative; almost anything can be tied to the enhancement of pastoral ministry.
- Choose a Bible passage and imagine what songs or musical score you might use with it.
- It's your turn. . . .

Once the mind is turned to pray and play, the world of "just being" is a never-ending, important place to spend time. Here are several suggestions about time spent just being. And for those with a limited budget, none is expensive. Since the number forty is the biblical metaphoric number for escaping into the wilderness, here are forty suggestions to help with stress or overwork:

1. Keep a journal of the day and make sure it includes the highlights, as well as the oddest things you saw.
2. Make a romantic phone call to someone you love and share an unexpected coffee break, or lunch, or dinner.
3. Visit an art museum.
4. Use an hour or a day for physical activity. If you love a particular sport, then join a team and dream of becoming a professional athlete.
5. Walk up to total strangers and tell them they're special. Watch for their reaction.
6. Schedule a lesson on a favorite musical instrument, or take dancing lessons.
7. Take a walk with someone you love.
8. Write a note to a friend telling why he or she is so wonderful.
9. Visit the library and read a book of humor.
10. Go for a walk in the woods or on the beach, or take stop, look, and listen moments. Make time to pay attention to the smallest things around you.
11. Do deep-breathing exercises or breath prayers.
12. Watch a YouTube video of a favorite musical group.
13. Visit a pet store or zoo.
14. Download musical instrument apps on your smart phone, play your favorite music, and add a special tech sound to the songs.

15. Volunteer as a family—not as the church, but for your own well-being—at a soup kitchen or food pantry.
16. Take a bike ride.
17. Read to a child.
18. Keep a large ball of clay nearby so you can play with it.
19. Take a close-up picture of everyday objects and then have others guess what each object is.
20. Clean something.
21. Take a one-day vacation.
22. Take steps to a healthier diet.
23. Start and end your meditative times with prayers of thanksgiving.
24. Call up a friend and ask him or her to tell you a joke.
25. Work on a crossword puzzle or play Scrabble with a friend.
26. Immerse yourself in water: take a swim, shower, or get into a whirlpool.
27. Read or listen to a book.
28. Garden or build something.
29. Bake something, or make a gourmet meal using leftovers.
30. During the holidays, create traditions that are fun and even outlandish—the craziest outdoor lights, the funniest tree ornaments, the oddest gift wrap.
31. Run outside, and jump up and down shouting, "Hurrah for God!"
32. Take an object and think about ten uses for it.
33. Send a contribution to a favorite charity.
34. Download apps that play restful sounds so they're at the ready when you need them.

35. Make passionate love with your spouse.

36. Carry a small sketch tablet with you, and, regardless of your ability, stop and sketch something you see. It will either inspire you, or make you laugh.

37. Plan to take a picture of the same spot at least once a week and see what changes take place.

38. Learn skills that make children laugh, such as magic or balloon animals.

39. Visit a bakery or fragrance store and smell the different products, or go to a restaurant and order something you never tried before.

40. Flip through an old scrapbook or photos.

41. Number forty-one is all yours. Dream, think creatively, do something that makes your heart dance or makes others smile or laugh.

You might ask, why this is such an important chapter? It's simple. Unless we live and minister with an open jar mentality, the joys of ministry will be lost. We will be too controlling of our ministry and the parishes we serve. Remember, if we don't loosen our grip, there's a good chance we'll lose our grip. The calls of ministry are many and the saints with whom we carry out Christ's ministry have many hopes, dreams, and even misconceptions. The truth is that unless we stay fit and faithful in body, mind, and especially Spirit, the Body of Christ we lead will be unfit for the journey of faith that we are called to take together. Dealing with haphazard theology requires the leadership of humble but energetic souls. May God bless us in our role as trainers in building up the Body of Christ. Christ's Body, the church, needs our physical energy and spiritual muscle to lift it up to where its members can gain a glimpse of the promised new heaven and new earth. The realm of God is here and now. Let us be the catalyst for taking the lid off so the church may become all that God intends it to be. Again, to God be the glory!

Inspiration

He who binds to himself a joy
Does the winged life destroy;
But he who kisses the joy as it flies
Lives in eternity's sun rise."

—WILLIAM BLAKE[1]

Prayer

God who calls us to tasks and challenges which seem beyond our capabilities and our depth of faith, help us to remember that we are not You, but that we can infuse Your will into our chaotic and peace-seeking world. Humble us when hubris overtakes us, and remind us that we don't have to do it alone. In all things, use us, use us, use us. In the Head and Heart of the Body's glorious name we pray this. Amen.

Postscript

A Good Word for the Local Church

An Apologetic but Not an Apology

It should now be unmistakably clear that I have a love affair with ministry in the local parish setting. We who are called to lead here are involved in profoundly meaningful work, and we should feel extremely blessed. I share with you a blog entry I wrote in response to those who are in attack mode when it comes to organized religion. Amid the foibles of organized religious practice and its struggles to emerge relevant to the ever-changing societal realities that arrive daily, there has been and always will be a need for what the church has historically been at its core and will need to be in the future. So my colleagues in local church leadership, I offer a good word to affirm and support why we have chosen to follow this mysterious yet intensely human being called Jesus.

I guess I have grown tired of the continual articles about faith is good/organized religion is bad journalistic efforts. It seems that an increasing number of people who say they hold to a faith-based perspective on life are offering demonstrative critiques of organized religion as found in the institutional church. Church bashing is increasingly in vogue. During my lengthy journey as an ordained minister serving for over thirty-five years in local churches, I have seen some of the less-than-Christian behavior that the faith-without-religion critics exhibit as they justify being unaffiliated. Still I must offer a good word for organized religion's basic unit of operation. It has always been my contention that the church doesn't receive the immense credit it deserves for its role in society—in the past and in the present. So I offer, without apology, an apologetic for the church.

The local church is the place where unique and diverse community is encouraged and fostered. While many churches lack racial-ethnic diversity as we define it today, it is still the place where young children, inquisitive teenagers, young and middle-aged parents, singles and couples, and seasoned citizens meet and greet and share their life stories. It is the place where seeking souls from across the economic spectrum sit side-by-side in the worship of the One who tears down the dividing walls. It is increasingly the place where people of different racial, cultural, and sexual-orientation backgrounds study the Bible together and work for the social welfare of those in greatest need. There are very few places in our society where people of different ages, economic circumstances, and racial and cultural backgrounds gather. Very few other organizations and institutions bring such diverse people together in search of the meaning of life. Not even the educational system—particularly with regard to diversity—can claim to be the place for building community.

The local church is the place where preventive holistic healthcare is always available. Whether it is the wisdom shared about living a fulfilling life through words spoken from a pulpit; sharing life's trials with someone during a fellowship hour or in a pastor's office; or community support in a time of illness or bereavement, the church is a primary healthcare provider. I cannot imagine how many times I have seen a word spoken, an embrace offered, and a counseling insight shared where some form of emotional, spiritual, or relational healing has taken place. Visiting the sick; communicating with the lonely; welcoming with equal love and care each person regardless of their status in the world's eyes; offering a space and a place for organizations that bring wholeness to the addicted and conflicted—that is the essence of the local church I know. You see, all this is accomplished with simple acts of goodness that bring no fanfare, no headlines.

The local church is a place that calls us to remember and to serve those in greatest need in the wider world. While attending to the well-being of its community, it also challenges those who dare to hear the Gospel call to think globally and to offer not just heart but hands in service to those in greatest need. It offers hands-on opportunities to experience the wider world and to work for changing the forces that cause oppression and division in the global community. It is a place that comforts our hurting souls and disquiets us from becoming too comfortable in a world where so many suffer. The church, particularly my United Church of Christ, has historically been the catalyst for societal action in the areas of quality education, racial and ethnic discrimination, women's and sexual-orientation equality and rights, quality healthcare, and so much more. Again, the church goes about its outreach and justice ministries seeking little public recognition.

The local church is a place where eternal values are taught. The church does offer a constant reminder of the values that are important for the salvation of our souls and the world. Yes, sometimes it's fair to criticize the church as being down in trivial and strident judgment. I once told a parishioner who asked one Sunday morning about the many facets of my job that I must remind all who will hear, including myself, of compassion, grace, forgiveness, kindness, patience, and humility. All these form a truly good and blessed life. All of us regularly need a refresher course in holy living and in values education.

And maybe the complaint by many faith-without-church advocates that "the church is filled with hypocrites" is yet another reason why the church is so valuable and essential. We need a place in the world that offers grace and calls for repentance. When remembering my childhood church, I recalled the funeral of one older member who constantly complained about almost everything the church did and supported. Still, at his funeral, the pastor, while acknowledging some of the man's shortcomings, said that he had been a good man and a child of God. Maybe the church's chief gift to the world is to welcome soiled and broken souls—all of us—with a word of grace and, when necessary, a loving call for repentance. In my ministry I have believed it to be my role to seek the God-ness and the good inside of the most cantankerous and mystifying souls who crossed my path. The church is a place of grace, and grace again. Where else is such compassion offered?

Maybe it is the other-centeredness of the church that keeps those seeking individualized salvation from entering into Christian community. I have a personal belief that in our ADD, "me-first" world many critics of the institutional church have not given participation in a community of faith a fair chance. The church must always be seeking relevance in every age. But also those desiring the benefits the local church offers must take time to study and examine the life-enhancing realities that being part of a true community of soiled saints has to offer. It is time that the "churched" speak out without apology about the blessings of being part of that community of seeking souls that is called the local church.

Appendix A
Weekly Pastoral Care Contact Checklist

Week of ____________________________

Contact Codes

IP —in person	**EM** —email
BP —by phone	**G** —group gathering
SN —**s**nail mail	**LC** —lay contact / other

1. Healthcare / Hospital
   ☐ *Names, date, form of contact, and information to remember*

2. Homebound / Long-Term Convalescent Care
   ☐ *Names, date, form of contact, and information to remember*

3. Crisis Intervention / Bereavement Contact or Follow-Up
   ☐ *Names, date, form of contact, and information to remember*

4. Counseling Contacts
   ☐ *Names, date, form of contact and information to remember*

5. Visitor Follow-Up / Potential New Member
   ☐ *Names, date, form of contact, and information to remember*

6. General Contact
   - ☐ *Names, date, form of contact, and information to remember*

7. Visitations such as at workplace, school
   - ☐ *Names, date, form of contact, and information to remember*

8. Attendance at Member Significant Events: anniversaries, birthdays, special recognitions, sporting events, activities in which they have a special role
   - ☐ *Names, date, form of contact, and information to remember*

9. Unexpected Contacts—such as at meetings and social events
   - ☐ *Names, date, form of contact, and information to remember*

10. Special resource contacts—written and shared through mass communication—Bible Study as comfort, prayers to inspire, blogs to uplift, worship bulletin inserts, etc.
    - ☐ *Type of resource, primary audience, distribution date*

Other Weekly Pastoral Care Notes:

Appendix B
Worship Planning Funnel

Follow prompts from the top to bottom of the funnel! Write notes inside or outside of the funnel. The object of this worship planning resource is to first open the minds of the planners and then distill the information into a cohesive, dynamic worship experience.

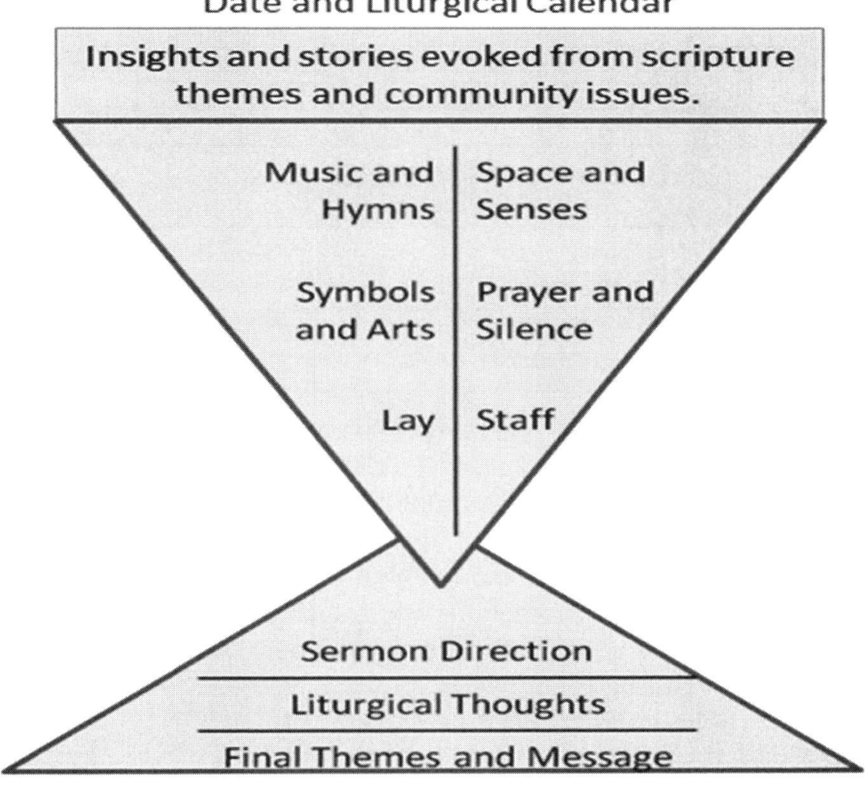

Appendix C
Educable Moment Exercise

The Moment / The Event / Other
Pay Attention to the Moment Sensory Information
Mind Information—What Were You Thinking at That Moment? Oddities About the Moment (If it's odd it might be from God!)
Your Feelings in the Moment How might others who were part of the moment be feeling?
Faith Tie-Ins / Scripture
Life Lessons / Insights

Educable Moment Exercise

The above guide is to be used as a faith-development exercise resource. You may wish to reflect on any moment in your life or community or on a worldwide event. This resource challenges the seeker to concentrate fully on any one moment or event, such as a surprise moment in the day, an interaction at the office, a moment of service at a soup kitchen, or a current event. Follow prompts from the top to the bottom. Take notes on where the process leads you.

Appendix D
Getting Started in Inclusive Youth Ministry

1. Begin with a prayer for discernment by the planning team.
2. Remember youth ministry is more than a youth club. Involve the youth in all aspects of church life. If you count numbers, count youth group members plus every youth who is involved in some facet of the church's ministry.
3. Youth have busy schedules; don't expect all of them to participate in all of the church's potential youth activities.
4. Select youth leaders who are youth-friendly but not overgrown teenagers. Age is irrelevant—respect for youth, energy, and maturity are the characteristics of a successful youth leader. Naturally a comfort in relating life to faith is essential.
5. In an inclusive youth ministry, begin with personal invitations for involvement in all aspects of the church's ministry: lay readers, musicians, artists, childcare assistants. If necessary, create a need for their inclusion by creating a need that matches their interests / talents.
6. To start a youth group:

   a. Begin with the strongest age group you have that is in middle school.

   b. While youth don't necessarily want their parents too heavily involved, occasionally ask parents to help out or host events.

   c. Try to build a program around the youths' interests, not the leader's.

   d. Be consistent with meeting times; start small and build.

   e. Remember hands-on wider mission outreach is attractive to youth.

7. A faith-based spiritual component should be part of all youth ministries. It can be as overt as group Bible study (it must be energetic and relevant) or as subtle as signs on the wall with spiritual messages that lead to questions. You might text information that can begin a dialogue through technology. Use of age-appropriate case studies is a great catalyst for lively discussion. When possible, use youth culture interests—music, games, arts, and sports—to stimulate faith talk.
8. Communicate, communicate, and communicate. Keep in contact with them in person and through the multiple forms of social media.
9. Keep alert to community issues that are affecting them.
10. Support them wherever they are, such as at school athletic and arts events.
11. Build a basic library of youth resources, much of which can be found on the Internet and is downloadable.
    a. Youth-oriented Bible study
    b. Fun and community building games
    c. Youth-focused meditations and prayers
    d. A church youth ministry journal, whether online or in print and mailed journal form.
12. Attend a conference about designing, building, and leading youth ministry.
13. Be available for one-on-one ministry. Build a youth advisor team.
14. Remember wider church and judicatory resources.

Appendix E
Church Growth Checklist

(*A coalescence of strategic information from Chapters 5 and 11*)

- The Community outside Your Church
  - ☐ What do people outside of your church think or say about it?
- The outer appearance of your church and property; what does this say to the community about your congregation?
  - ☐ What might be done to alter the visual image of the church/property?
- How would you describe the neighborhood within a mile radius of your church?
  - ☐ What is the demographic makeup?
- How would you describe the area: Is it urban downtown, residential, rural for instance?
- When people enter the building and go to various administrative, worship, and program spaces, what would be their first impression?
  - ☐ Ease of finding their way around the building . . .
  - ☐ General attractiveness and maintenance . . .
- In light of these findings, what might be some initiatives that need to be addressed?
- The product
  - ☐ What are the current demographics of your church?

- ☐ Is the Spirit alive and is the community excited about the ministry?
- ☐ Has the mission of your church been defined?
- ☐ Since worship is usually the first encounter a visitor has with the church, how would you describe the level of energy found during worship?
- ☐ Are your ministry programs attractive?

◆ Marketing

- ☐ How are you visible in the community?
- ☐ When people move to your community, how do you make contact with them?
    - Through community welcome organizations?
    - Print media?
    - Technology? Website, Facebook, other social media?

◆ Training the Sales Reps, the Laity

- ☐ How to be a good neighbor?
- ☐ How to invite?

◆ The Liturgy of Worship Welcome

- ☐ In the worship bulletin or through technology, is there a statement about the essence of the church and a welcome to visitors?
- ☐ How are visitors greeted as they enter? Are they identified in worship? Are there ways to gather information about visitors in worship?

- ❑ Does the liturgy allow the visitor to easily become part of the worshipping community?
- ❑ Are members of the congregation ready to recognize and feel comfort in the ministry of welcome?
- ❑ Are there after-worship exit strategies?
- ❑ Are there after-church social time strategies in place?
- ❑ Is there a follow-up contact plan?

◆ Sacrament and Rite Evangelism

- ❑ Is the importance of having a church home stressed in pre-baptism and pre-marital counseling?
- ❑ Are there plans in place for church members to be a welcoming presence at the sacraments and rites of the church?
- ❑ Are those seeking these church ministries given information about all church activities?
- ❑ Is there follow-up contact with those who have participated in the rites and sacraments?

◆ Outside Visibility

- ❑ Is outside signage used to attract the attention of those passing by the church?
- ❑ Are some outdoor programs held where they are visible to those passing by the church?

◆ Brokering the Building

- ❑ Is there information about the church visible to outside organizations using the church building?

- ☐ Are there ways of covenanting with these organizations to get information about the church to their participants?

- ◆ Staff and Lay Leader Visibility in the Community
  - ☐ Are staff members involved in organizations that might attract members of those organizations to the church?
  - ☐ Are lay leaders and other members comfortable talking about their church in community organizations in which they are involved?
  - ☐ Does the church have a presence in community activities such as holiday celebrations and special community events?

- ◆ Outside-the-Box Strategies
  - ☐ What unique church growth strategies might you consider if "anything goes"? Keep it Christian, moral, and definitely fun!

- ◆ After this reflection, what are some new church growth initiatives your church could take on?

Appendix F

A Sample Narrative Budget

- Include a cover letter that explains how a narrative budget is constructed.
    - Faith greeting
    - Narrative budget reflects how the dollars and cents budget is used in programs.
    - Percentage of each line item is broken down into program areas of ministry.
- The narrative budget also helps to see the details of exactly what is being accomplished in ministry. It helps to clarify the day-to-day activities of the church.

Cover Letter

Dear Church Family Members,

What a blessed church we are! Our ministries are energized and growing. The following is a narrative budget that illustrates the vitality of our church's witness and helps to show what percentage of our budget we are spending in each area of our ministry. It offers a clear vision for our ministry and our priorities in our witness for Jesus Christ.

Worship:
26 percent

Our worship is at the core of our life together. Our clergy spend many hours in research and writing for more than fifty-four sermons and the planning of over sixty-three regular and special worship services a year. Our music ministry offers three choir programs that enhance our celebration of the Good News. Secretarial time spent preparing bulletins, using reams of paper and many copier resources, undergird our worship ministry. Since we like to worship in warmth and with adequate light, there are utilities bills that must be paid.

Faith Development through Christian Education: 16 percent

You've seen an increasing number of children in our church school program and a church calendar filled with more Bible studies and intergenerational programs that nurture our faith development. Our youth ministry has added a new tech dimension allowing them to interact through social media. For curriculum expenses and the costs associated with having an exciting director overseeing our children's ministries, we spend an estimated $185 per year on each participant in our church school program. Additionally we provide adult study resources and economical but essential technology.

(This section could be further broken down into children, youth, intergenerational, adult.)

Ministries of Pastoral Care: 19 percent

Over 750 in-person and phone visits, including, home, hospital, homebound, care facilities, funeral follow-up, and new member visits; over 150 hours of pre-marital, baptism, family, and crisis counseling; the purchase of and writing of care support resources, which are at the heart of our caregiving ministry.

Wider Mission: 12 percent

We do go to the entire world. Our local mission supports:

____

and our national and global efforts support:

____ .

Our personal connection to Phyllis Jones, our missionary in Botswana, our two youth and one intergenerational mission trips as well as the cost of the food we cook for the local soup kitchen, just touch the tip of the iceberg of our wider mission efforts. And let us not forget the community care organizations that use our church building.

Evangelism / Church Growth: 7 percent

We are experiencing a steady growth in membership. Much of that has come from our media visibility in the community and our constantly improving website and expansion of our social media ministries. By a vote of the church council, we have contracted a person who can assist as need for our small, but energetic staff, to enhance our community and social media presence. An up-to-date website is essential if we are to attract visitors. We also hope to purchase a new outdoor church sign in the coming year

Unallotted Buildings and Grounds: 15 percent

While we have tried to include many of the buildings and grounds costs under the above categories, some are difficult to designate to any one program area. There is grass to be cut and snow to be removed and the unexpected maintenance crises to be addressed. There is also the one-time refurbishing of our nursery and narthex.

Administrative and Other Miscellaneous: 5 percent

As you can see from our narrative budget, we are a church on the move but also with new challenges to address. We go out in hope knowing that God will use our material resources to bring the witness of new life in Christ to our church and wider communities.

If you have any questions about our church and its finances or about this narrative budget do not hesitate to contact :

____

Notes

Introduction

1. Thomas James Mullen, *Mountaintops and Molehills: Essays in Haphazard Theology* (Waco, Tex.: Word Books, 1981), 41.

2. Henri Nouwen, *Creative Ministry* (New York: Image, 1991).

Chapter 1

1. Roy M. Oswald and Otto Kroeger, *Personality Types and Religious Leadership* (Washington, D.C.: Alban Institute, 1988).

2. Anthony De Mello, *One Minute Wisdom* (New York: Image, 1988).

3. Harvey Cox, *The Feast of Fools: A Theological Essay on Festivity and Fantasy* (Cambridge, Mass.: Harvard University Press, 1969).

Chapter 2

1. Douglas Harper, *Online Etymology Dictionary*. http://etymonline.com.

2. Ronald Rolheiser, *Against an Infinite Horizon: The Finger of God in Our Everyday Lives* (New York: Crossroad, 2002), 11–12.

3. American History, Suite 101, Vancouver, BC. http://suite101.com.

4. Stanley Hauerwas and William H. Willimon, *Resident Aliens: A Provocative Christian Assessment of Culture and Ministry for People Who Know Something Is Wrong* (Nashville: Abingdon, 1989).

5. Rolheiser, *Against an Infinite Horizon,* 34.

6. Mary Oliver, "When Death Comes," in *New and Selected Poems* (Boston: Beacon, 1992).

Chapter 3

1. Wikipedia, "Juggling World Records." http://en.wikipedia.org/wiki/Juggling_world_records.

2. Christine Rosen, "The Myth of Multitasking," *New Atlantis: A Journal of Technology and Society* (Spring 2008).

3. Wikipedia, "Juggling World Records."

4. David J. Wolpe, *Teaching Your Children about God: A Modern Jewish Approach* (New York: HarperPerennial, 1995)

Chapter 4

1. Wes Seeliger, *Western Theology* (Atlanta: Forum House, 1973), 21.

Chapter 5

1. Michael Watkins, quoted in Martha Lagace, "A Fast Start on a New Job," *Working Knowledge* (Harvard Business School), November 10, 2003.

Chapter 6

1. Thomas Lynch, *The Undertaking: Life Lessons from the Dismal Trade* (New York: W. W. Norton, 1997), 56.
2. Frederick Buechner, cited in Frederic Brussat and Mary Ann Brussat, *Spiritual Literacy (*New York: Scribner, 1996), 91.

Chapter 7

1. Isaac Asimov (1920–92), U.S. science and science-fiction writer.
2. Abraham Joshua Heschel, *I Asked for Wonder: A Spiritual Anthology,* ed. Samuel H. Dresner (New York: Crossroad, 1983).
3. Thomas Lynch, "The Dead and Gone—Ritual of Mourning," *Christian Century* (November 14, 2001), 5.

Chapter 8

1. Anthony De Mello, *Taking Flight* (New York: Image, 1988), 21–22.
2. Ted Loder, *Guerillas of Grace: Prayers for the Battle* (Minneapolis: Fortress, 2005), 31. Used with permission.
3. Mahatma Gandhi, *The Essential Gandhi: An Anthology of His Writings on His Life, Work, and Ideas,* ed. Louis Fischer (New York: Vintage, 2002), 2.
4. Dan Kimball. *The Emerging Church: Vintage Christianity for New Generations* (Grand Rapids: Zondervan, 2003), 7–8.
5. Richard J. Foster. *Celebration of Discipline: The Path to Spiritual Growth* (San Francisco: Harper, 2002), 173.

Chapter 9

1. See, for example, "A Bible in the Hand Still May Not Be Read," *Baptist Standard,* December 4, 2000.
2. Stephen Prothero, *Religious Literacy: What Every American Needs to Know—and Doesn't* (San Francisco: Harper, 2007).
3. Charlotte Hays, "Why Sunday Schools Are Closing," *Wall Street Journal,* June 26, 2009.
4. Theodore Roethke, "The Waking." http://www.poetryfoundation.org/poem/172106.html.
5. Evelyn Underhill, quoted on the Spirituality and Practice website. http://www.spiritualityandpractice.com.

6. Holly Chatterton Allen, "Nurturing Children's Spirituality in Intergenerational Christian Settings," cited in John Roberto, "Best Practices in Intergenerational Faith Formation," *Lifelong Faith* (Lifelong Learning Associates), Fall–Winter 2007.

7. Leonard Sweet, *Learn to Dance the Soul Salsa: 17 Surprising Steps for Godly Living in the 21st Century* (Grand Rapids: Zondervan, 2000).

Chapter 10

1. Ochristian.com, http://christian-quotes.ochristian.com.

2. Rick De Marinis, http://www.idlehearts.com.

3. Ronald Rolheiser, *Against an Infinite Horizon: The Finger of God in Our Everyday Lives* (New York: Crossroad, 2002), 126.

Chapter 11

1. Diana Butler Bass, *The Practicing Congregation: Imagining a New Old Church* (Washington, D.C.: Alban Institute, 2004).

Chapter 12

1. Douglas John Hall, "Stewardship as Human Vocation," Stewardship of Life Institute (September 7, 2010), www.stewardshipoflife.org.

2. Leonard Sweet, *Learn to Dance the Soul Salsa: 17 Surprising Steps for Godly Living in the 21st Century* (Grand Rapids: Zondervan, 2000), adapted.

Chapter 14

1. Christopher Tate, Associate Pastor, Second Congregational Church, Greenwich, Connecticut; e-mail to the author, November 2, 2012.

2. Sherry Turkle, "The Flight from Conversation," *New York Times*, April 21, 2012.

3. Diane Ackerman, *A Natural History of the Senses* (New York: Vintage, 1991), 123.

Chapter 15

1. William Blake, "Eternity," http://www.amblesideonline.org/Blake.

Bibliography

Ackerman, Diane. *A Natural History of the Senses.* New York: Vintage, 1991.

Allen, Holly Chatterton. "Nurturing Children's Spirituality in Intergenerational Christian Settings." Cited in John Roberto, "Best Practices in Intergenerational Faith Formation." *Lifelong Faith* (Fall–Winter 2007).

American History, Suite 101, Vancouver, B.C. http://suite101.com.

Asimov, Isaac. http://www.goodreads.com.

Baptist Standard, "A Bible in the Hand Still May Not Be Read," December 4, 2000.

Bass, Diana Butler. *The Practicing Congregation: Imagining a New Old Church.* Washington, D.C.: Alban Institute, 2004.

Blake, William. "Eternity." http://www.amblesideonline.org.

Buechner, Frederick, cited in Frederic Brussat and Mary Ann Brussat. *Spiritual Literacy.* New York: Scribner, 1996.

Carey, William. Quoted on Ochristian website.

Cox, Harvey. *The Feast of Fools: A Theological Essay on Festivity and Fantasy.* Cambridge, Mass.: Harvard University Press, 1969.

De Marinis, Rick. Quoted on Idlehearts website: http://www.idlehearts.com

De Mello, Anthony. *One Minute Wisdom.* New York: Image, 1988.

De Mello, Anthony. *Taking Flight.* New York: Image, 1988.

Foster, Richard J. *Celebration of Discipline: The Path to Spiritual Growth.* San Francisco: Harper, 2002.

Gandhi, Mahatma. *The Essential Gandhi: An Anthology of His Writings on His Life, Work, and Ideas.* Edited by Louis Fischer. New York: Vintage, 2002.

Hall, Douglas John. "Stewardship as Human Vocation." Stewardship of Life Institute, September 7, 2010.

Harper, Douglas, *Online Etymology Dictionary.* http://www.etymonline.com.

Hauerwas, Stanley, and William H. Willimon. *Resident Aliens: A Provocative Christian Assessment of Culture and Ministry for People Who Know Something Is Wrong.* Nashville: Abingdon, 1989.

Hays, Charlotte. "Why Sunday Schools Are Closing." *Wall Street Journal,* June 26, 2009.

Heschel, Abraham Joshua. *I Asked for Wonder: A Spiritual Anthology.* Ed. Samuel H. Dresner. New York: Crossroad, 1983.

Kimball, Dan. *The Emerging Church: Vintage Christianity for New Generations*. Grand Rapids: Zondervan, 2003.

Loder, Ted. *Guerrillas of Grace: Prayers for the Battle.* Minneapolis: Fortress, 2005.

Lynch, Thomas. "The Dead and Gone—Ritual of Mourning." *Christian Century*, November 14, 2001.

Lynch, Thomas. *The Undertaking: Life Lessons from the Dismal Trade.* New York: W. W. Norton, 1997.

Mullen, Thomas James. *Mountaintops and Molehills: Essays in Haphazard Theology*. Waco, Tex.: Word Books, 1981.

Nouwen, Henri. *Creative Ministry.* New York: Image, 1991.

Oliver, Mary. "When Death Comes." In *New and Selected Poems.* Boston: Beacon, 1992.

Oswald, Roy M., and Otto Kroeger. *Personality Types and Religious Leadership.* Washington, D.C.: Alban Institute, 1988.

Prothero, Stephen. *Religious Literacy: What Every American Needs to Know—and Doesn't.* San Francisco: Harper, 2007.

Roberto, John. "Best Practices in Intergenerational Faith Formation." *Lifelong Faith* (Fall–Winter 2007).

Roethke, Theodore, "The Waking," http://www.poetryfoundation.com/poem/172106; from *Collected Poems of Theodore Roethke.*

Rolheiser, Ronald. *Against an Infinite Horizon: The Finger of God in Our Everyday Lives.* New York: Crossroad, 2002.

Rosen, Christine. "The Myth of Multitasking." *New Atlantis: A Journal of Technology and Society* (Spring 2008).

Seeliger, Wes. *Western Theology.* Atlanta: Forum House, 1973.

Sweet, Leonard. *Learn to Dance the Soul Salsa: 17 Surprising Steps for Godly Living in the 21st Century.* Grand Rapids: Zondervan, 2000.

Turkle, Sherry. "The Flight from Conversation." *New York Times*, April 21, 2012.

Underhill, Evelyn. Quoted on Spirituality and Practice website. http://www.spiritualityandpractice.com

Watkins, Michael. Quoted in Martha Lagace, "A Fast Start on a New Job." *Working Knowledge,* Harvard Business School, November 10, 2003.

Wikipedia, "Juggling World Records." http://en.wikipedia.org/wiki/Juggling_world_records

Wolpe, David J. *Teaching Your Children About God: A Modern Jewish Approach.* New York: HarperPerennial, 1995.